SIMPSON

The publisher and the University of California Press Foundation gratefully acknowledge the generous support of the Simpson Imprint in Humanities.

The Kingdom of Rye

California Studies in Food and Culture

DARRA GOLDSTEIN, EDITOR

The Kingdom of Rye

A BRIEF HISTORY OF RUSSIAN FOOD

Darra Goldstein

UNIVERSITY OF CALIFORNIA PRESS

University of California Press
Oakland, California

This book was prepared with the assistance of the Multimedia Art Museum, Moscow.

Library of Congress Cataloging-in-Publication Data
Names: Goldstein, Darra, author.
Title: The kingdom of rye : a brief history of Russian food / Darra Goldstein.
　　Other titles: California studies in food and culture; 77.
Description: Oakland, California: University of California Press, [2022] | Series:
　　California studies in food and culture; 77 | Includes bibliographical references
　　and index.
Identifiers: LCCN 2021045269 (print) | LCCN 2021045270 (ebook) |
　　ISBN 9780520383890 (hardback) | ISBN 9780520383906 (ebook)
Subjects: LCSH: Food habits—Russia—History. | Food—Russia—History. | Cooking,
　　Russian—History. | Russia—Social life and customs.
Classification: LCC GT2853.R8 G65 2022 (print) | LCC GT2853.R8 (ebook) |
　　DDC 394.1/20947—dc23/eng/20211015
LC record available at https://lccn.loc.gov/2021045269
LC ebook record available at https://lccn.loc.gov/2021045270

Manufactured in the United States of America

31　30　29　28　27　26　25　24　23　22
10　9　8　7　6　5　4　3　2　1

For my sister, ARDATH WEAVER, whose creativity and support have guided me all these years

И год хорош, коль уродилась рожь.
If the rye ripens, it's a good year.

RUSSIAN SAYING

Дорого бы я дал за кусок черного хлеба!
What I wouldn't give for a piece of black bread!

ALEXANDER PUSHKIN, *A Journey to Arzrum* (1835)

Contents

Illustrations

MAP 1. Russia and places mentioned in this book.

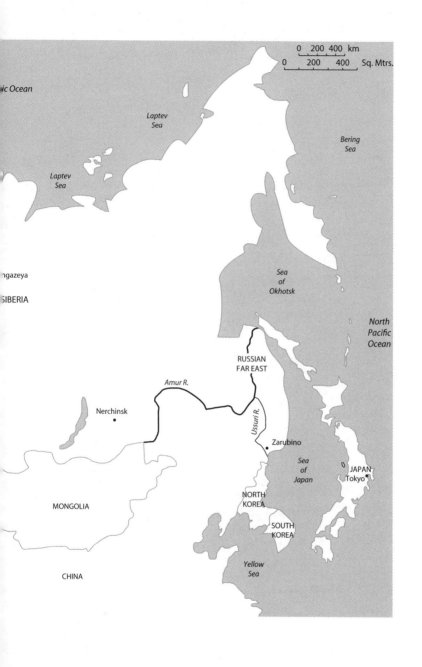

Arctic Ocean

Laptev
Sea

Bering
Sea

Laptev
Sea

0   200 400 km
0   200   400   Sq. Mtrs.

ngazeya

SIBERIA

Sea
of
Okhotsk

North
Pacific
Ocean

RUSSIAN
FAR EAST

Amur R.

Nerchinsk

Ussuri R.

Zarubino

Sea
of
Japan

JAPAN
Tokyo

MONGOLIA

NORTH
KOREA

SOUTH
KOREA

CHINA

Yellow
Sea

Preface

In my family, Russia was a place to escape from. My grandparents had fled in the early twentieth century—I never knew exactly when—and they refused to share stories of their past. So the country loomed large in my imagination. I tasted it in my grandmother's beet kvass, in her sorrel soup, in her stuffed cabbage.

In college, I decided to study Russian to learn more about this beguiling place. In those days we weren't taught oral proficiency; we entered the language through grammar and literature. I struggled through texts that refused to yield their meaning; then suddenly I'd happen upon a passage describing food, and the language would magically open up to me. These passages occurred surprisingly often. I absorbed the sentences first as sensations, even before I understood the actual words. Only after I'd figuratively savored the dishes did I look up the unfamiliar words in the dictionary to memorize their exact meaning.

One literary meal led to another. My language skills improved, and I longed to visit Russia. The mere thought of my traveling there horrified my grandmother, but in 1972 I went nonetheless. My first breath of Soviet air immediately dispelled any romance: the place smelled of overcooked cabbage. The gray food I encountered matched the dingy surroundings. This wasn't the French-inflected haute cuisine I had encountered in nineteenth-century literature; nor was it the rustic food of the peasantry. This was Soviet food in an era when few ingredients were available. On that first visit I didn't taste the famous fish pie, *kulebiaka*, so erotically described by Chekhov, or the plump pancakes known as *bliny* that Gogol's hero Chichikov downs three at a time after dipping them in melted butter. But I thrilled to the flavors of coriander-studded rye bread, to open-faced buns filled with sweetened farmer's cheese, to Siberian dumplings laced with vinegar and mustard, to half-sour cucumbers and golden, brined cloudberries. Only later, after I broke through the surface (and the rules about what foreigners could and could not do), did I finally begin to experience all the vibrant flavors of Russia.

Once I got to graduate school, I intended to write my dissertation on food in Russian literature. But I was ahead of the times. In 1974 hardly anyone in American academia took food seriously—certainly not my Stanford professors, who maintained I would have no future with such a trivial pursuit. So I focused instead on Russian modernist poetry (which I don't regret). But I never abandoned my subversive idea of writing about Russian food. As I studied for my qualifying exams, I jotted down every reference to food I encountered over two centuries of Russian literature. Many of these quotations eventually found their way into my first cookbook, *A la Russe: A Cookbook of Russian Hospitality,* which came out in September 1983, just as I started teaching Russian literature at Williams College. The book may have begun as a metaphorical thumbing of my nose at the stuffy attitudes of my professors, but it became a response to the year when I'd taken a break from grad school, working instead for the United States Information Agency in Russia. I served as a guide for the exhibition Agriculture USA, an outcome of the 1958 cultural agreement between the US and the USSR. The exhibition's presentation of American agricultural bounty was not apolitical. It was a finger in the eye to a country suffering severe food shortages heightened by the Cold War. I had a fleeting but nasty encounter with the KGB, made worse by a debriefing by US State Department security, and by the end of my ten-month stint, I was ready to give up Russian studies—no matter that I'd already invested so much. But something pulled me back, and that something was Russian hospitality. Ordinary people asked me to dinner. We crowded around tiny tables, eating with mismatched plates and forks in tiny, rudimentary kitchens, and the food was delicious. My pursuit of things Russian was saved by the generosity of all the people who opened their homes to me, often at considerable risk, to share whatever they could put together from the scarce resources at hand. My book was my thank-you note.

Over the years, as I traveled throughout the Soviet Union and then Russia, my interest in Russian food only deepened. I was still working in archives, researching Russian poetry, but my real aim was to understand Russian food culture—the origins of dishes, the role of the traditional Russian stove, the superstitions surrounding preparation, the influence of the Orthodox Church, gender roles in the kitchen, etiquette at the table, the introduction of foodstuffs from East and West and how Russians adapted them to their own taste. It was a pleasure and a passion to uncover Russia's most elemental flavors, the ones that stretch back over a thousand years, to try to define the basics of the cuisine.

My research eventually took me to tiny villages in the Russian north, where cooks still prepare food in masonry stoves and each year put up liters of foraged and cultivated fruits and berries for the unrelenting winter ahead. I described these foods in my most recent cookbook, *Beyond the North Wind: Russia in Recipes and Lore,* which appeared in 2020. The book you now hold in your hands is its more historical and ethnographic sibling. Tracing Russian culinary culture from its pre-Christian beginnings up to the present day, *The Kingdom of Rye* represents a culmination of my lifetime of thinking about Russia and the marvels of its food. And at a time when tensions once again divide Russia and the West, cultural understanding becomes all the more crucial.

A note on transliteration and translation: Throughout the book I have used the modified Library of Congress system, except for proper names that have a different conventional spelling, such as Metchnikoff. Unless otherwise noted, all translations are mine.

Introduction

Nineteenth-century Russia was overflowing with gingerbread—gingerbread in all shapes and sizes, figured, sculpted, and stamped. If we're to believe the authors of an 1838 guidebook, the town of Gorodets alone produced a staggering 360,000 pounds of gingerbread each year. Gingerbreads (*prianiki*) were highly localized, with numerous cities and towns laying claim to the very best. Vyazma *prianiki* were bite-sized, the dough so sticky with honey that it had to be pounded with wooden mallets and tempered for days—sometimes weeks—until it reached the right consistency for baking. The honey provided flavor, of course, but it also kept the cookies moist for months. Connoisseurs knew not to bite down on them but to let each cookie melt in the mouth to release the honey's taste. Supersized gingerbreads from Gorodets were baked in large loaves embossed with designs made by pressing the dough into carved wooden boards. These *prianiki* could be six feet in length and weigh up to thirty-six pounds. So famous was the gingerbread baked in Tver that it was exhibited at the 1876 Philadelphia Centennial International Exposition, where it appeared alongside inventions by Alexander Graham Bell and Albert Einstein. This gingerbread won a bronze medal for its many varieties and the originality of its designs.

Russian gingerbread started out simply as a mixture of rye flour, honey, and berry juice that was left to ferment for a few days before baking. Because honey accounted for almost half of the mixture, the cakes were known as "honey bread" until spices were added some centuries later. Increasingly, bakers used gingerbread as a medium to display their artistry. The earliest gingerbread, molded into symbolic three-dimensional shapes, gave way to decorated rectangular loaves. The gingerbread boards used to press patterns into the dough became an important expression of Russian folk art, one that reflected evolving trends in subject matter, from familiar creatures like roosters and sturgeon to complex narrative scenes scored into individual squares that could be broken off. The most extravagant *prianiki* were decorated with gold leaf.

This progression from simple to excessive, turning the mundane into the fanciful, can be seen as typically Russian. That bakers would lavish so much effort on a food unnecessary for survival is a telling example of the way in which traditional Russian culinary culture responds to hardship—to a harsh climate, repressive regimes, and austere religious strictures—punctuating frugality with flashes of extravagance.

Most of the Russian populace lived their lives on the edge, teetering towards hunger and dependent on an annual harvest that could be destroyed by untimely frosts, drought, hail, insects, or commissars. During tsarist times, the peasants' lack of capital meant that they couldn't buy food when their own crops failed, even though grain and bread might be in abundance nearby; in Soviet times, food often rotted in the fields for lack of spare parts

FIGURE 1. Wooden gingerbread board from the northwestern city of Vologda, made in the second half of the nineteenth century. Incised patterns allowed bakers to create charming designs that appeared in bas-relief on the baked gingerbread. The best boards were made from hardwoods like pear and birch into which fine details could be carved. At baking time the stiff gingerbread dough was pressed into the well-oiled board and then turned out onto a metal sheet before being slid into the oven. The rooster shown here, with its mix of abstract and organic forms, is typical of Russian gingerbread folk art. Collection of the Kunstkamera, Saint Petersburg. © MAE RAN 2021.

for harvesting machinery, or arrived at its destination spoiled because of unreliable distribution systems. Russia has endured far more than its share of famines. In the twentieth century, the worst periods of hunger—the Volga famine of 1921–22 during Russia's civil war, the brutal collectivization campaign in 1932–33, and the siege of Leningrad during World War II—were caused not by natural forces but by social upheaval and cynical political determinations.

Even in years unmarked by particular calamity, Russian peasants went hungry, or at least went without, and scarcity became the mother of their inventiveness. While ever mindful of the dark historical record, this book celebrates the Russian people's ingenuity in dealing with hardship and the gustatory delight that can emerge from privation. Adversity for Russians has given rise to a remarkably vibrant repertoire of foods. When I experience the pungency of garlic and horseradish, the intensity of lacto-fermented vegetables and fruits, the sour tang of black bread and the hearty bite of whole grains, the woodsy flavor of mushrooms, and the dusky notes of cloudberries, I am reminded of the Russian ability to preserve and to persevere.

These are the flavors of the land, transformed through fermentation, slow cooking, culturing, and baking into dishes that are greater than their individual parts. If deprived English speakers live from hand to mouth, Russians live "from bread to kvass"— kvass being a fermented beverage made from stale rye bread. Bread, the mainstay of the diet, was considered sacred even into modern times, and none ever went to waste. It was dried and fermented into effervescent kvass or layered as breadcrumbs in a pudding with puréed apples and a little honey. A sought-after confection known as Kaluga dough for its town of origin was made by simmering stale breadcrumbs in spiced honey syrup. Oats weren't just boiled into porridge; they were dried and roasted and pounded into a flour called *tolokno* that imparts a nutty flavor to pancakes and dairy dishes, or they were soaked to produce oat milk, more than a thousand years before it became trendy in Brooklyn. Buckwheat groats were mixed with sautéed chanterelles and onions, then garnished with brined lingonberries, in an early Russian version of a grain bowl. Even though the Russian table has been enriched by the introduction of new foodstuffs from both East and West, the flavors that typify the Russian palate have remained surprisingly constant: the tang of cultured dairy products like sour cream and yogurt-like *prostokvasha,* the bite of strong mustard and horseradish, the zing of fermented cucumbers and cabbage. If we think in terms of the anthropologist Sidney Mintz's "core-fringe" hypothesis—which holds that a culinary culture's "core," usually a bland, complex carbohydrate, is enlivened by bold accompaniments that constitute its "fringe"—we can see the inventiveness of ordinary Russians, who elevate core staples of Russian cuisine like rye, buckwheat, and oats with fringe complements of fermented and cultured foods. These additions add piquancy to starches while also providing necessary nutrients, often in the form of the probiotics we like to tout today.

Frequent famines helped to induce a certain fatalism among the Russian people, which in a cruel irony made hunger easier to endure: If the gods will it, our bellies will be full. If not, we'll manage somehow. After Russia accepted Christianity in 988, the Russian Orthodox church shrewdly turned privation into a virtue by designating nearly two hundred days a year as fast days. Prolonged fasts coincided with the agricultural seasons of greatest scarcity. But the Russian Orthodox calendar also evinced aware-ness of human nature. The stringent fasts were punctuated by feast days, so that there was always something to look forward to. On these feast days a cook might bake a sumptuous pie, or some gin-gerbread, or simmer a soup with a little meat. For most of the year, though, the peasantry awaited relief, or else dreamed of the *skatert'-samobranka,* the self-spreading tablecloth of Russian fairytales. Such culinary utopias were common throughout medi-eval Europe (the most famous being the land of Cockaigne), but Russia's version was in a way more immediate: if you could just get your hands on the magical tablecloth and unfold it, lavish delica-cies would instantly appear.

Dreams of cornucopia weren't just a thing of fairytales and the past. Well into the late twentieth century, the Soviet government trumpeted abundance to create an illusion of material well-being. Shop windows featured artfully arranged displays of canned goods that concealed the empty shelves inside. Moscow's handful of fancy restaurants triumphantly presented diners with oversized, leather-bound menus listing dozens of dishes when only a handful were ever available from the kitchen. The nightly news broadcasts ended with images of plentiful harvests playing across the screen, with wheat pouring through hoppers like waterfalls of golden grain—no matter that the government was often forced to import wheat from its political enemies to make sure there would be enough cattle fodder and bread. Foodstuffs randomly appeared and disappeared, and shopping took real talent. Even when virtu-ally nothing seemed to be available, almost everything could be had if you knew how to obtain it. And obtain it people did, putting together some of the most elaborate meals I've ever enjoyed—food shortages being a catalyst for creativity.

My introduction to the Russian table came through reading the alluring descriptions of food in Russian literature: Nikolai Gogol's four-cornered pie, so luscious it could make "a dead man's mouth water"; Chekhov's *kulebiaka,* a layered fish pie that's "appetizing, shameless in its nakedness, a temptation to sin." These enticements and others made me long to visit Russia, to taste its grand dishes. But when I finally got there, during the Cold War, I was shocked by the food deficits and indifferent cooking that defined Soviet reality. I tried to reconcile the delicacies I'd savored in my imagination with the everyday fare that sustained me, like *stolichnyi salat,* a pyramid-shaped potato, chicken, and vegetable salad dripping with mayonnaise. That near-daily salad, one of the few constants on Soviet menus, proved both a comfort and an unexpected rabbit hole. Little did I know at first bite that this "capital salad" was a bastardized version of the elegant salade Olivier first introduced to fashionable Muscovites in the 1860s. Nor did I realize that behind each bowl of borscht, each spurt of butter from artfully prepared chicken Kiev, lay a hidden and often complex history.

Culinary practices are as dynamic as languages, continually changing in relation to the social context in which they are performed. New foods are introduced, old dishes fall out of favor; kitchen technologies change as new dietary trends emerge. Thus the idea of a stable national cuisine can seem contrived. But, as with languages, we can trace words back to roots. We can identify representative ingredients and a unique grammar of techniques, or marked philosophies of dining, or certain distinctive flavor profiles that typify a cuisine. It is tempting to tell the culinary story of Russia in terms of dualities and easy juxtapositions: scarcity and abundance, feasting and fasting, poverty and wealth, restraint and excess, modesty and flamboyance. And such pairings can reveal a lot about social structures and about the way food is consumed. But they can't begin to communicate what is, to me, most crucial: food's taste and texture, the technologies of preparation, the aesthetics of the table, and, perhaps above all, its cultural resonance and the emotional value of traditional flavors, how people know who they are by what they eat together.

Writing about food calls for an appreciation of food's sensory qualities, whether it's the heady fragrance of Antonov apples in autumn or the visceral smell of pig's feet simmering into the meat aspic called *studen*.' What equivalencies are there between an aristocratic table, laden with flowers and shimmering with candles *à la russe*, and a peasant family's rough board, upon which a communal pot of wild mushroom and barley soup has been set? Where but in Russian literature can you find that nineteenth-century prototype, the superfluous man, bemoaning the emptiness of life even as he reaches for another piece of pie as if for the embodiment of truth? And who is to say that the superfluous man isn't right to find truth materialized in sensory delight? This domestic history of Russian food offers a look into people's daily lives, to serve up a history that originates from the wooden spoon rather than from the scepter.

1   *The Land and Its Flavors*

The old man crumbled some bread into his cup, mashed it with the stem of his spoon, poured on some water from his whetstone case, sliced some more bread and, after sprinkling it with salt, turned to the east to pray.

LEV TOLSTOY, *Anna Karenina*

At the heart of any traditional Russian meal lies black bread, a loaf of dense sourdough rye. The old man's simple dinner above is a dish known as *tiurya*, which consists of breadcrumbs usually soaked in kvass, a fermented beverage made from rye bread. *Tiurya* is essentially bread on bread, sometimes with a little onion added for flavor. So ingrained was rye in the Russian diet that by the late nineteenth century, 30 to 60 percent of the country's arable land was annually planted in this crop, leading to a veritable "kingdom of rye." The peasants expressed reverence for their rye bread by holding the loaf close to the chest and slicing it horizontally toward the heart. Wasting breadcrumbs was considered a sin, and even into the late twentieth century, entire cookbooks were devoted to using leftover black bread.

Rye bread is highly nutritious and slow to digest, and therefore good for keeping hunger at bay. More than a nutrient, bread is also a sacrament. That the old man in *Anna Karenina* says a prayer before his meal isn't surprising, as most Russian peasants were devout Orthodox Christians. But the fact that he turns to the east reveals something more about the Russians and their world. Early Slavs envisioned the sun as the eye through which God looked at the world, and even after the advent of Christianity, they continued the act of devotion. In a holdover from pagan times, the old man faces the direction of the rising sun, as if asking the sun god, Dazhbog, for a blessing. And to this day Russians make blini, their beloved pancakes, golden and round in the image of the sun, as they did over a thousand years ago, when they baked them on hot stones at the vernal equinox to coax the sun to return after a long, dark winter. By following tradition they pay homage, even if they no longer consciously connect the round pancakes with the god of the sun.

The numerous gods and spirits that ruled the early Slavic world were not always benign. For Russians, nature is not just landscape or backdrop; it is a vital, often unpredictable, force. A forest *leshii* could withhold prey from hunters. The spirits of trees felled for timber lived on in cottage walls. House and barn spirits protected families or wreaked havoc at will, ensuring well-being or fomenting disaster. Even today, Russians' frequent foraging for nature's gifts—the mushrooms, berries, and wild herbs gathered from forest, meadow, and swamp—reflects a spiritual need, a deep-seated urge not just to be outdoors, but to become one with nature, breathing in what Vladimir Nabokov describes in *Speak, Memory* as the "special boletic reek which makes a Russian's nostrils dilate—a dark, dank, satisfying blend of damp moss, rich earth, rotting leaves."

Staple Foods

Russia straddles two continents and constitutes about one-seventh of the Earth's entire land mass. Any overview of the country's cuisine necessarily elides the vast ecological differences in the country's various regions. In central Russia, the great swath of chernozem—extraordinarily fertile soil stretching into the Eurasian steppes—allows for productive agriculture, especially the cultivation of grains. To the south, the temperate climate enables the growing of heat-loving crops like eggplant and wine grapes. The diet in the north is more limited, with a greater reliance on fish and hearty grains. But it is still possible to identify a spectrum of flavors and taste preferences that characterize the Russian table.

Russia's north is home to the taiga, vast boreal forests where travelers once reported "great pools" and "lakes" of honey in hives swarming with wild bees. Honey is Russia's age-old sweetener, originally mixed with rye flour and berry juice to make gingerbread and employed to preserve fruits and vegetables for long keeping. It formed the basis of the aromatic meads at which the Russians excelled. On a seventeenth-century visit to the northern city of Arkhangelsk, the English horticulturalist John Tradescant proclaimed Russian honey the best in the world. Honey was the dominant sweetener well into the nineteenth century, until the rise of the sugar-beet industry made sugar more affordable.

The forests also provided abundant mushrooms and berries to supplement a meager diet that revolved around grains—primarily spelt, barley, oats, millet, and buckwheat in addition to rye. Grains were most often turned into porridge or gruel, and particularly into a dish known as *kisel'*. For oat *kisel'*, whole oats were soaked in water and then strained. The starch-rich liquid (the original oat milk) was left to ferment for several hours, often with a heel of rye bread added to speed up fermentation. The oat milk was then gently heated until it set to a solidity anywhere from a slightly thickened liquid to a sliceable block. Well into the twentieth century *kisel'* remained a staple of fast-day meals, especially when made from dried pea flour and drizzled with hempseed or flaxseed oil. *Kisel'* is still popular today, though it is now made mainly from fresh fruit and enjoyed as a beverage. The appeal of this privation food persists beyond times of privation.

Oats also yield *tolokno,* a finely textured, nutty-tasting flour whose simplicity belies the arduous labor once required to make it. Whole oats were soaked for twenty-four hours (preferably in a sackcloth bag moored to the bottom of a fast-flowing river or stream) until they began to germinate. Then they were slowly steamed for twenty-four hours in an earthenware pot in the great Russian masonry stove. Only then were they dried and husked before being pounded—never ground—into flour. *Tolokno* is mixed with water for porridge, sprinkled onto blini, or turned into the ultra-rich pudding *dezhen',* made with sour cream and farmer's cheese (*tvorog*).

Foraged bounty was enjoyed in season, though most was preserved for times when fresh food was scarce. Mushrooms were salted or dried or, less often, marinated in vinegar; berries were boiled with honey into jam, pressed into juice, fermented into kvass, or dried into fruit leather. Orchard fruits were also prized, especially apples and cherries. Apples were often lightly brined for long keeping or turned into a kind of fruit leather that over time evolved into today's ethereal *pastila.* Until cabbage began to be cultivated in Kievan Rus' (the earliest Russian state) late in the ninth century, turnips were the main garden crop. The onions and garlic that now typify the Russian kitchen were also introduced around that time, and even though their cultivation was slower to take hold, by the time of the Earl of Carlisle's visit to Muscovy (the late-medieval Grand Principality of Moscow) in 1663, his secretary noted that "Onions and Garlick are so common amongst them, especially in their Lents, that one needs go no further than his Nose for information." Other staples closely associated with Russia—potatoes and sunflower oil—were much later additions to the pantry.

Throughout the Middle Ages many new foods, including spices, were carried along the trade routes and introduced from the Byzantine Empire, enabling affluent diners to enjoy lemons and season their meat, fish, soup, and sweets with saffron, cloves, nutmeg, cinnamon, cardamom, and powdered ginger. Greek monks and Black Sea merchants brought additional foodstuffs, most notably buckwheat, known colloquially in Russian as *grechka,* "the Greek one." It soon became Russia's most beloved kasha, or porridge. The sibilant-rich Russian saying "Shchi da kasha, pishcha nasha" (Cabbage soup and kasha, that's our food) places these two dishes at the heart of Russian cuisine. Cabbage soup carries particular symbolic weight. The word *shchi* can be traced back to an Old Slavonic word meaning "sustenance," itself derived from the Sanskrit word *suta. Suta* was the juice extracted from soma, a plant offered up in ancient India's Vedic sacrifices. This juice was considered sacred, an essential libation that conferred the energy of the sun. If we follow this derivation and its line of thinking, we can see that the sacred essence of *shchi* lay not in the meat that over time became the object of desire, but in the liquid, whether in the form of brine from fermented cabbage or the braising liquid from fresh cabbage soup.

For Russians, dinner without soup doesn't quite add up to a meal, and for much of the populace, soup often *was* dinner. The repertoire of Russian soups is extensive, from hearty vegetable-and-grain-based *pokhlyobka* (wild mushroom and barley) to the elegant fish soup made with sterlet and champagne beloved of the aristocracy. Soup making highlights Russian ingenuity. Many soups, like *rassol'nik,* are enhanced by the addition of pickle brine to yield the sour taste that Russians love and to ensure that the flavorful brine doesn't go to waste. One of the most cherished Russian soups is a clear fish broth known as *ukha,* whose only constant ingredients are fish, water, salt, and pepper. Cooks vary the flavor profile by choosing different types of fish and differing herbs and spices. *Ukha* was once categorized by color, with the black variety containing bottom-feeding fish like carp, the white version brimming with pike or perch, and the red (etymologically related to the word "beautiful" in Russian) containing the prized sturgeon. The fish broth could also be given a colorful moniker according to how it was seasoned: yellow had saffron; black contained pepper, cinnamon, and cloves; and white had very few spices at all.

Perhaps most revealing of this penchant for variety are the small bites that always accompany soup. Even today, soup is never served alone but always with bread, hand pies, dumplings, croutons, or other tidbits; tradition dictates what goes best with each type of soup. Even within these categories are many variations. Croutons intended for puréed soups differ in shape and cooking method from those designed for clear bouillons; croutons for spicy soups require the addition of cheese and cayenne. Elena Molokhovets's classic nineteenth-century cookbook, *A Gift to*

FIGURE 2. Vladimir Sokolaev, *Butter Week Pies*, 1976. The pre-Lenten holiday of Maslenitsa, or Butter Week, is a sendoff to winter, when vast quantities of the pancakes known as *bliny* are traditionally consumed. There are other pleasures as well. During the weeklong celebration, streets are filled with vendors selling all manner of foods, such as hot *pirozhki* or handpies, shown here steaming in the frosty air of Mayakovsky Square in the Siberian city of Novokuznetsk. Collection of the Multimedia Art Museum, Moscow.

Young Housewives, devotes an entire chapter to 170 recipes for soup accompaniments, many of them for hand pies.

Pies are, in fact, another defining feature of Russian cuisine, and at grand banquets they constituted a separate course. The varieties are near endless, from the hand pies known as *pirozhki* to extravaganzas like *kulebiaka*—a fish pie, adopted into French haute cuisine as coulibiac, that contains layers of salmon and sturgeon, thin pancakes, buckwheat groats or rice, mushrooms, onions, and herbs—and *kurnik,* a tall, conical pie filled with chicken, thin pancakes, mushrooms, rice, and hard-boiled eggs. Pies were most often baked right on the hearthstone of a masonry stove, but smaller ones could be fried in butter or goose fat—or, on fast days, hempseed or flaxseed oil.

Native riches included abundant freshwater fish in rivers and lakes, and wildfowl in meadows and swamps, although access was not equal across social classes. The gentry had both the leisure and the means to devote to hunting and fishing. The nineteenth-century writer Sergei Aksakov's *Notes on Fishing* and *Notes of a Provincial Wildfowler* are extraordinary not just for the practical knowledge he shares but also for his keen observations and rapturous sense of belonging to nature. By contrast, the peasants who made up 85 percent of the population in the nineteenth century were often denied permission to hunt or fish on landowners' property, and they couldn't enjoy the hazel hen, snipe, and burbot that were considered great delicacies. Burbot liver was especially prized for the unctuousness it lent to soups and pies.

Such inequalities in wealth, land ownership, and access to foods, both native and imported, make it difficult to describe a monolithic Russian cuisine, particularly after the reign of Peter the Great (1696–1725), whose eighteenth-century reforms caused the culinary lexicon to change drastically. As French became the language of choice among the elite, French haute cuisine conquered wealthy kitchens. Even such an ostensibly Russian dish as beef Stroganoff is nothing less than a classic *ragoût* in Russian guise, with sour cream used in place of sweet cream and the addition of Russia's beloved mushrooms. The peasant diet was spared these foreign intrusions.

Most Russians subsisted on bread, porridge, and soup, supplemented by whatever they managed to forage. Wealthier classes, such as well-to-do merchants, were renowned for the lavish, sometimes bawdy, restaurant meals they hosted, and more prosperous peasants who owned a cow consumed an array of dairy products, including the familiar *tvorog* (farmer's cheese) and *smetana* (sour cream). However, the vast majority of the population had to be more resourceful, compensating for the monotony of their diet through the intrinsic deliciousness of its ingredients. Russian black bread is highly aromatic, with a wonderful sour tang; buckwheat porridge is made earthy by adding onions and wild mushrooms. It can be enriched with a fatty, garlicky slice of *salo* (cured fatback similar to Italian *lardo*), which also seasons soups, while dill brightens them. Even the nobility, with their private French chefs, betrayed a weakness for traditional Russian foods, interspersing menus featuring consommé with crêpes and *boeuf à la cuillère* with *kulebiaka* and Russian-style sturgeon.

Ubiquitous taste preferences include, above all, a love of the sour, basically expressed in the classic rye loaf and lacto-fermented cucumbers and cabbage; the sweet and sour, such as onions cooked slowly in honey until caramelized into a condiment known as *vzvar;* and the acid invariably added to borscht in the form of beet kvass, vinegar, lemon, or, more recently, tomatoes. Lewis Carroll, the author of *Alice's Adventures in Wonderland,* visited Russia in 1867, accompanying his friend, the theologian Henry Liddon, who wanted to promote the reunification of the Anglican and Russian Orthodox churches. In his journal Carroll described a meal at a roadside inn: "This place was also remarkable for our first tasting the native soup, Щи (pronounced shtshee), which was quite drinkable, though it contained some sour element, which perhaps is necessary for Russian palates." Russians also love the salty and pungent; horseradish and strong mustard are favored condiments. Contrary to stereotype, when Russian food is well prepared, it is anything but bland.

"The Earth Is Our Mother, Bread Is Our Father"

White bread has made significant inroads into the Russian diet, but the word *bread* still evokes the dense, dark, sourdough rye loaf Russians have eaten for centuries. Rye bread is more wholesome than wheat, thanks to rye's copious amounts of B-complex vitamins and gut-friendly microbes that arise from lacto-fermentation, as well as the fact that rye starch breaks down into sugars more slowly than that of wheat, producing the lower insulin response that makes rye bread so filling. While Russian peasants were unaware of these fine points of food chemistry, they knew how to stay strong and understood that they couldn't live without their black bread. Neither could Russian elites, even though they could also enjoy fine white bread. The poet Alexander Pushkin, in his *Journey to Arzrum* (1835), relays the complaint of his friend Lieutenant-Colonel Pyotr Vasilevich Sheremetev, who had recently returned from a tour of duty in France: "It's tough living in Paris, brother. There's nothing to eat, you can't get black bread."

A 1626 ukase by Tsar Mikhail Fyodorovich regulating the weight and price of bread lists twenty-six different varieties of rye loaves. The cost depended on how finely the flour had been milled and bolted and how much sourdough and salt were added to the dough. The most inexpensive loaves, made of coarsely bolted flour, were dark in color and quite sour, since they contained more sourdough than the finest "white" rye loaves (*sitnye*). These dark loaves furthermore contained no salt. They were enormous, weighing in at some twenty pounds; fine rye loaves were smaller. Notable among the latter was the enriched "boyar" loaf, made with finely bolted flour, butter, slightly soured milk, and spices. The royal court enjoyed even smaller "stamped" (*basmannye*) loaves, baked on site by special bakers. These beautiful loaves were named after the *basma,* a metal plate bearing the image of the khan that was a legacy of the Mongol occupation. Like Uzbek *naan* even today, these breads were stamped with a decorative pattern on top made by a pronged instrument. For all breads, a special cadre of inspectors, the so-called bread police (*khlebnaia pristava*), ensured that standards were met, on penalty of punishments that ranged from a hefty fine to public flogging.

For all of its close association with Russia, rye was an almost accidental crop that originated as a weed in the wheat fields of southwest Asia. When farmers discovered that this lanky grass was much hardier than wheat—able to withstand heavy frosts, drought, and poor soil—they encouraged its cultivation. By the early tenth century rye had made its way to Rus', and within another century it had become the predominant grain. Russian peasants subsisted largely on rye products. They ate the whole grains as porridge and milled them into flour for bread. Stale rye bread was turned into kvass, a drink as nourishing as it is refreshing. Leftover mash from the kvass making was used as a starter for more black bread, thus completing the circle.

It is no wonder, then, that Russians felt such reverence for rye bread, believing that not only their health but also their fortunes depended on it. Their veneration was both religious and superstitious. The alchemy of bread was awe-inspiring: the starter fermented, alive with bubbles, until the heat of the masonry stove— itself a life-giving force—transformed the simple mixture of flour and water into a solid loaf. In the Russian Orthodox church, bread is the intermediary between God and man, as symbolized by the ritual of communion, and its relation to the divine inspired numerous superstitions. Someone who dropped a piece of bread had to kiss it after picking it up and either eat it right away or throw it into the fire. Woe to anyone who left an uneaten piece of bread on the table, an act that was sure to cause illness. No crumb was to be wasted. One superstition held that the devil gathers up all the bits of bread that a person discards over his lifetime. After that person dies, if these bits of bread weigh more than he does, then the devil will take his soul.

Magical thinking also surrounded the actual baking of bread, to ensure that the loaves rose properly. So strong was its symbolism that bread was used to augur fertility and abundance. Brides were sometimes made to sit momentarily on the tub that held fermenting dough, and bread was crumbled over newlyweds, as well as over the plot of land where a cottage was to be built. A loaf was often placed in the cradle with a newborn baby. If a hailstorm threatened, bread and its accouterments—the dough trough and oven peel—were carried outside to protect the crop.

Traditional Beverages

Fermentation lies at the heart of Russia's traditional beverages. From the earliest times the Russians have tapped birch trees in spring and enjoyed the light, refreshing drink called birch juice, which they also fermented into the lightly alcoholic *beryozovitsa*. Another fermented beverage, and Russia's original favorite, is mead, made from honey. The finest mead (*stavlenyi myod*) is barrel-aged like wine to achieve a mellow yet complex flavor. Monks were renowned for the fruit meads they made by mixing raw honey with tart fruit juice—including raspberry, lingonberry, and cherry—and then allowing the liquid to ferment before transferring it to oak barrels, where it aged for a minimum of five years and ideally fifteen or twenty. Waiting decades for properly aged mead wasn't to everyone's liking, and by the sixteenth century people had figured out that by adding hops and yeast to the honey, they could brew mead (*varyonyi myod* or *medovukha*) that matured in only a few weeks. Other honey drinks included *syta,* a mixture of water and honey served either hot or cold. The hot, spiced honey drink *sbiten',* once sold by street hawkers from samovar-like urns, remains popular today.

Although both *beryozovitsa* and mead fell out of fashion, another family of ancient drinks survives in the form of beer and kvass. Early Russians brewed a light beer without hops, called *braga.* There was also *perevar,* a brew of honey and beer considered valuable enough to be used in the payment of tributes. By the sixteenth century, vodka had begun edging out these native drinks, with detrimental effects. When construction began in 1703 on Peter the Great's new city of Saint Petersburg, the tsar took note of workers' lack of industry. He had been impressed by the industrious dockworkers he encountered on a visit to London, where workers enjoyed beer. So he provided imported English beer for the architects and engineers, and beer from local breweries for the regular workers. After Peter's death, beer once again fell out of style until it was revived by the Prussian-born empress Catherine the Great. For her wedding to Tsar Peter III, Catherine's father sent a present of the renowned beer from Zerbst, her native town, and during her reign (1762–96), beer imports rose tenfold. Catherine also promoted the dark, rich stout still known today as Russian imperial stout. Yet among the lower classes, a taste for inexpensive, locally made beer never caught on.

Why drink bad beer when one can enjoy kvass, an effervescent, mildly alcoholic beverage most commonly made from grain?

Typically prepared from stale sourdough rye bread that is left to ferment with honey, kvass, a Russian original, resembles a kind of small beer without hops. Traditional red kvass was made by slowly steaming malted grains, flour, and water in the masonry stove until the mixture took on a deep, rich color and flavor. To make white kvass, the same ingredients were left to ferment without heat. Robust red kvass was often flavored with hearty aromatics like mint and St. John's wort, while the more delicate white kvass could be infused with violet roots, raisins, and dried apples. Kvass can also be fermented from fruits and vegetables, some of the finest being made from raspberries and pears. Beet kvass makes an exceptionally flavorful base for borscht. In the countryside, kvass made a frequent appearance in the *banya,* the Russian sauna-style bath, not only as a refreshing drink after steaming, but also for dousing oneself with when there was no nearby ice-cold water to jump into. Using malted grains, Russians also made an especially fizzy kvass with the odd name of *kislye shchi,* literally "sour cabbage soup." Considered more elegant than basic kvass because of its extra sparkle, even as it was recognized as being deeply Russian, it often found a place on aristocratic tables and at theater buffets. In his prose fragment "Roslavlev," Alexander Pushkin describes how, in a newly nationalist impulse following Napoleon's invasion of Russia, Francophile high society "renounced Lafitte and took up *kislye shchi.*"

Having survived for centuries, kvass nearly met its match in 1974, when Soviet citizens got their first taste of Pepsi. PepsiCo had opened a production facility in southern Russia following a 1972 bilateral agreement stipulating that the company could bottle its drink from concentrate in the USSR in exchange for distributing Stolichnaya vodka in the US. Not to be outdone in the cola war,

УГОЩЕНІЕ НАПОЛЕОНУ ВЪ РОССІИ

FIGURE 3. I.I. Terebenov, *A Treat for Napoleon in Russia*, 1813. This caricature of Napoleon at the time of his defeat reveals a good deal about Russian food and nationalism. Napoleon has been stuffed into a vat of Kaluga dough, a beloved, sticky confection made of rye bread and molasses. A Russian soldier force-feeds him with gingerbread from the town of Vyazma, a famously long-lasting variety. A second soldier plies Napoleon with *sbiten'*, a hot spiced honey drink to which a third soldier is adding copious grinds of pepper. All three of these delicacies were metonyms for the Russian state. The rhyming quatrain beneath the image reads: "You grew tired of your own stuff;/You wanted Russian treats;/So here's some Russian sweets! Eat up and do not gag!/Here's some pepper *sbiten'*, drink up and don't get burned!" Collection of the State Historical Museum, Moscow.

Coca-Cola entered the Soviet market in 1979 with the introduction of bright orange Fanta, and Coke followed in 1985. These two American corporate giants continue to compete in Russia today, but their drinks have never supplanted kvass, which remains ubiquitous (even though its commercial versions taste nearly as sugary as Pepsi and Coke). Russians regard kvass as their national drink, part of their potable patrimony. Virtually every brand includes a tagline on the label stating that it has been made according to traditional Russian methods. This strong cultural identification has enabled kvass to endure throughout the ages and across social classes, despite trendy imports from the West. And in a further ironic twist, both Coca-Cola and PepsiCo launched their own signature brands of kvass in 2007. PepsiCo's version, Russian Gift, plays up Russian identity on its label by using the ornamental folk patterns of the *khokhloma* style, with painted berries, flowers, and leaves in brilliant tones of red, gold, and black.

Although widely considered to be synonymous with Russia, vodka was originally an outlier. Distilled rather than fermented like the drinks Russians were accustomed to, this spirit was a novelty. The exact moment and place of vodka's appearance in Russia remain uncertain; but whether it arrived from the south, through Crimea, or from Western Europe, its presence in Russia was documented by the fifteenth century. Vodka was originally intended for medicinal purposes and sold by apothecaries in tiny 4-gram portions, a far cry from today's generous 100-gram (3½-ounce) shots. Tsar Ivan IV (the Terrible) established the first state-run taverns, liberating vodka from the pharmacy, and domestic production began soon thereafter. Until the late nineteenth century, vodka was known as *goriachee vino* (burning wine) or *khlebnoe vino* (grain wine); the word *vodka* (an affectionate form of "water") is of relatively recent origin. But the word's intrinsically diminutive form reveals the fondness many Russians feel for this drink, which displaced the older, less potent potables.

Vodka began causing social problems almost immediately. Although the government regulated its production and sale, officials had little incentive to kill the cash cow that enriched the state coffers through hefty taxes. But drunken stupors had obvious ill effects on family life, worker efficiency, and military preparedness. Russia's various regimes have teetered ever since between lax and strict approaches to vodka. At times they have encouraged its consumption to build up the state treasury or dampen public unrest, to the point of banning temperance societies and exiling their proselytizers to Siberia; at other times they have curtailed access to vodka, as Tsar Nicholas I finally managed to do in August 1914, though prohibition resulted in increased mortality from the consumption of moonshine. The Soviet leader Mikhail Gorbachev's anti-vodka campaign in the 1980s led to popular discontent and arguably hastened the fall of the Soviet Union.

Partly because vodka was initially used to treat ailments, Russians have a long history of infusing the plain spirit with any number of healing herbs and spices. In a vivid passage from Nikolai Gogol's story "Old-World Landowners" (1835), Pulkheria Ivanovna describes the medicinal as well as sensory benefits of infused vodka: "This . . . is vodka infused with yarrow and sage—if someone's shoulder blades or lower back hurts, it helps a lot. This one is infused with centaury—if you have ringing in your ears or shingles on your face, it helps a lot. And this one is distilled with peach pits— have a glass, doesn't it smell divine?"

Some recommendations for infusions were quite elaborate. *The Gastronomes' Almanach* from 1852, a cookbook catering to the moneyed classes, instructs hosts to set out the following flavors for guests to enjoy: "white Seville orange, red Seville orange, bitter Seville orange, mint, almond, peach, spiced vodka, clove, raspberry, cherry, ratafia, Spanish spiced, Balsam, Danzig, rose, anise, wormwood, gold, cinnamon, lemon, caraway." The most distinctively Russian take on vodka might be *zapekanka,* vodka mixed with honey and spices and baked slowly in the oven to allow the flavors to infuse. A true test of manliness is the drink known as *yorsh,* named after the ruffe, a freshwater fish with spiny gills. If the English shandy is half beer and half lemonade, *yorsh* is more like the American boilermaker, containing beer and vodka in equal measure.

Trade Routes

Complicating our notions of Russia's historical isolation, trade routes crisscrossed the country, enabling the introduction of countless foods from the north and the south, as well as from the east and the west. Trade routes from Scandinavia to Constantinople developed around the end of the eighth century, long before Russia became a unified nation. One early route extended from Sweden via the Baltic Sea to the shores of what would become northwest Russia, where it took advantage of the region's vast network of rivers and lakes to reach all the way down to the Black Sea. Known as "the road from the Varangians to the Greeks" (the Varangians being the Vikings), this passage flourished until new routes were established by the Crusades. By the early tenth century the princes of Kievan Rus' had signed an agreement with Constantinople, the seat of the Byzantine Empire, that opened up even more possibilities for trade. In exchange for honey and furs, the Russians imported rice (which, until the mid-nineteenth century, they called "Saracen millet" [*saratsinskoe psheno*]), spices, and wines. In 1237 the Mongols invaded the Russian principalities. They restored ancient trade routes from China, along which noodles, fermented cabbage, and cultured milk products like koumiss—the mare's milk drunk by Turkic nomads (and by Tolstoy in his old age)—made their way. Some of the most basic food words in Russian, like groceries (*bakaleia*), dried fish (*balyk*), watermelon (*arbuz*), dried apricots (*kuraga*), and rhubarb (*reven'*), reveal Turkic roots, although some of these borrowings came later.

Russian trade expanded eastward, to the Volga River and beyond, during the reign of Ivan IV (1547–84). Commerce in spices increased, as did trade in dried rhubarb root, which became a lucrative export prized for its medicinal properties. Rhubarb's English name betrays its origins in *Rha barbarum*—from the old name for the Volga, Rha, coupled with the ancient belief in the barbarism that lay beyond the "civilized" world. From the Volga region, too, came sweet watermelons from Astrakhan and greater access to the extraordinary sturgeon and caviar from the Caspian Sea. Dried fruits were also introduced from the East, and Russians have used them deftly ever since. In affluent homes, Eastern methods for preserving root vegetables like carrots and radishes in sugar syrup became part of the culinary repertoire.

Toward the end of his reign, Ivan IV annexed Siberia, an act that gave Russia land on two continents, Europe and Asia. From this union came various types of boiled dumplings, such as *manty* stuffed with ground lamb and the beloved Siberian *pel'meni*, wonton-like pockets of dough filled with ground meat and onions. Though the origins of *pel'meni* are contested, they likely made their way from China to the area east of the Ural Mountains, where

Russians encountered them. Their name, literally "dough ears," comes from the language of the Komi-Permyak people who lived in that region. Enormous quantities of *pel'meni* were prepared at the onset of winter and kept frozen outdoors, ready for boiling into a quick meal. Tea from the Far East also arrived by way of Siberia, as a gift from the Mongol khan to Tsar Mikhail Fyodorovich, the first tsar of the Romanov dynasty, who reigned from 1613 to 1645. That gift turned Russia into one of the great tea-drinking cultures of the world, with the samovar, a brass urn for heating water, becoming a symbol of Russian hospitality.

Spices came to Russia via the northern branch of the Silk Road, the Black Sea in the south and, somewhat later, the port city of Arkhangelsk in the north. In 1555 the English import-export firm the Muscovy Company was chartered, with Sebastian Cabot (the son of John Cabot, who explored North America) installed as its first governor. Arkhangelsk, located where the Northern Dvina River flows into the White Sea, became a vibrant merchant town soon after its founding in 1584. Foreign ships filled the harbor, bringing luxury goods such as sugar, wines, rum, fruits, coffee beans, and spices. These goods were transported upstream along the Dvina and then overland to Moscow, a journey of nearly eight hundred miles that could take several weeks. For over a century Arkhangelsk remained Russia's only seaport, although it was ice-bound for half the year. Because the Gulf Stream warmed Norwegian waters in the Barents Sea, making fishing possible there year-round, the Russians traded Siberian grain for cod, haddock, salmon, and flounder. Trade thrived. Only after 1703, when Peter the Great established Saint Petersburg on the more temperate Baltic Sea, did Arkhangelsk fall into decline.

Though the routes that made up the Silk Road are familiar thanks to the romance of its textiles, spices, teas, and caravansaries, the lucrative trade in the north was equally significant. It included commerce between Norwegians and the local population of Pomors on Russia's northwestern coast that thrived until the 1917 revolution. In addition to engaging in localized coastal trade, the Pomors had begun carving out a river route from Arkhangelsk to the remote Siberian city of Mangazeya a century before the founding of Saint Petersburg. Like a Wild West trading center for furs and grain, Mangazeya was described in contemporary accounts as *zlatokipiashchii*—teeming with gold. The Pomors hoped to connect the city with the profitable Western European trade, but Tsar Mikhail Fyodorovich was so threatened by their entrepreneurial activity that he forbade it under penalty of death. By 1662 Mangazeya was deserted. All traces of the city eventually disappeared, to live on only in legend before being rediscovered in twentieth-century archaeological digs.

Peter the Great's reign considerably broadened Russia's palate—or at least the palates of those who had money to spend on expensive imported food. He developed the old Astrakhan highway, one of the northern routes of the Silk Road that stretched 1,800 miles from the city of Astrakhan at the mouth of the Caspian Sea, along the high banks of the Volga, and on to Moscow via that great river's tributaries. (His daughter, Empress Elizabeth, turned this highway into an imperial "fruit express" that carried fresh produce from Astrakhan all the way to the Saint Petersburg court in specially equipped carts. During blizzards, villages along the route would "chime the storm" by ringing the church bells to guide travelers—an aural, inland counterpart to lighthouses.)

In 1712 the imperial court moved from Moscow to Saint Petersburg, and in 1713, ten years after the city's founding, construction began on Gostinyi dvor, the commercial center, whose design incorporated a canal so that boats could unload their wares on site. The provisioning of Saint Petersburg was shaped not only by the city's geography but also by its demographics. Peter the Great offered foreigners generous benefits to come to his city and help develop the new capital's industry and its arts and social institutions. Petersburg's significant foreign population also Westernized the city's eating habits, and previously unknown foods like waffles and artichokes found a warm reception. Meanwhile, the Russians whom Peter had sent abroad to advance their education returned with new tastes along with new skills. Seeking more variety in their diet, they began to import novel foods.

As the Russian Empire continued to expand in the nineteenth century, parts of Central Asia and the Caucasus came under its control. Although these regions provided Russia's major cities with warm-climate foodstuffs, distinctive dishes from these places were slow to become part of the culinary lexicon. Those adoptions occurred only under Soviet rule with its trumpeting of "the brotherhood of all peoples." This propagandizing promoted a culinary nationalism through which new dishes and techniques were adopted into Russian cuisine, especially from Georgia and Uzbekistan. Georgian chicken *tabaka* (garlicky flattened chicken) became a reliable restaurant standard whenever chicken was available. Also popular were Georgian *khachapuri* (cheese bread), Uzbek *plov* (rice pilaf), Azerbaijani *lyulya-kebab* (ground lamb kebabs), and especially *chebureki*, fried Crimean meat pies, which became a beloved fast food. The Ukrainian boiled dumplings known as *vareniki* were enthusiastically embraced, especially when filled with sour cherries, as was *salo,* the Ukrainian national snack of spiced, cured pork fatback. Vil'yam Pokhlyobkin's famous 1978 cookbook, *The National Cuisines of Our Peoples,* claimed all of these dishes and more as part of the Soviet patrimony. Yet a close reading of his text reveals a colonialist attitude and condescension towards the culinary practices of non-Slavic peoples, even as their foods were eagerly co-opted. Many of the new dishes brought into the Russian repertoire during the Soviet years became inexpensive street food accessible to nearly everyone.

Culinary Practices

Russia is not a quick-cooking culture. The nature of traditional Russian cuisine was in large part determined by the design of the masonry stoves that had come into use by 1600. These massive structures for both cooking and heating could measure up to two hundred cubic feet, occupying a good quarter of the living space in one-room peasant cottages. They were built of bricks or stone rubble covered with a thick layer of whitewashed clay. (For heating, wealthy families also had so-called Dutch stoves faced with beautiful tiles—even utilitarian objects provided an opportunity to display their prosperity and aesthetic taste.) Unfortunately, far too many peasant cottages fell into the category of "black," meaning their stoves had no chimneys, and much of the smoke lingered in the air, to detrimental effect. More affluent peasants lived in "white" cottages in which the smoke was vented through a chimney.

Unlike other countries where fuel was scarce, resulting in the adoption of quick cooking methods, Russia boasted extensive

FIGURE 4. A.A. Belikov, Russian masonry stove with cooktop in the cottage of the well-off peasant I.I. Pavlov, 1925. The built-in cooktop with its own fire-box signals the affluence of the owner, as do the decorative tiles affixed to the whitewashed surface; neither feature was typical of the most traditional stoves. The sleeping platform, here used for storing pots, is visible behind the chimney. Collection of the Kunstkamera, Saint Petersburg. © MAE RAN 2021

forests and thus plentiful firewood. The thick walls of the stove retained heat very well, and many of Russia's most typical dishes result from this property. When the stove was newly fired and very hot, with embers still glowing at the back of the hearth, cooks placed breads, pies, and even blini in the oven to bake. It took two to three hours to bring a cold oven up to temperature. Experienced cooks inserted a piece of paper to determine when the oven was ready for baking, based on how quickly the paper browned and burned. So central was bread to Russian life that oven temperatures were often described in relation to bread baking: "before bread, after bread, and at full blast" (*vol'nyi dukh*). As the heat began to diminish, other dishes took their turns: grain porridges that baked to a creamy consistency, followed by soups, stews, and vegetables, which were cooked slowly in bulbous earthenware or cast-iron pots. When the oven temperature had fallen to barely warm, it was just right for culturing dairy products and drying mushrooms and berries. During the winter, the stove was fired once or twice a day, and in summertime, only as needed for baking.

At the rear of the masonry surrounding the traditional Russian stove, high above the floor, is a ledge. This *lezhanka* (from the verb "to lie") was the warmest spot in the peasant cottage. There, the elderly or infirm could find comfort, and children could laze like the beloved folk figure Emelia the Fool. Most stoves also provide recesses for storing food, kitchen equipment, and wood, as well as niches for drying mittens and herbs. The oven cavity itself is massive, large enough for uses well beyond cooking. The stove could become a makeshift *banya* when planks were set up along the hot interior walls of the oven, and this cleansing ritual endured well into the twentieth century. It usually took place on a bread-baking day, when the oven was already heated, and was considered especially beneficial when steam from the hot water released the aroma of medicinal herbs. Some Russians took a "bread bath," believed to have healing powers, by using diluted kvass instead of water to create the steam. In some regions of Russia women crawled into the oven to give birth, since it was the most hygienic place in the cottage. Beyond such practical uses, the stove played a highly symbolic role in Russian life, demarcating the traditional female and male spheres, with the cooking area to the left of the hearth and the icon-dominated "beautiful corner" to its right. And not surprisingly, given its importance in providing sustenance, heat, and health, the stove was believed to hold magical powers beyond the alchemy of transforming dough into bread. Mothers would sometimes place sick infants on bread peels and ritually insert them three times into the oven in hopes of curing them.

The masonry stove prevailed in Russian households both rich and poor until the eighteenth century, when Western-style ranges and the new equipment they required gradually came into use. Many Russian stoves were modified to include stovetop burners in addition to the oven, and in some households a cooktop range superseded the stove entirely. Saucepans and griddles largely replaced the customary earthenware and cast-iron pots perfect for slow cooking in the Russian stove. Cooktops also affected the way ingredients were prepared. In kitchens that could afford meat, large joints for roasting or braising gave way to butchered cuts like steaks, filets, and chops that could be prepared à la minute, often in more elaborate, if less natively Russian, recipes.

The Russian stove released deep, mellow flavors through slow cooking even as its low heat enabled culturing and dehydration, which produce intensified flavors that also characterize Russian cuisine.

Steaming and Slow Cooking

Russia's most distinctive method of cooking, based on the properties of the masonry stove, is a process known as *tomlenie,* a cross between steaming and braising. Steaming retains nutrients in a way that boiling cannot, while slow braising coaxes out flavor. Raw ingredients are layered in a pot with as little liquid as possible. The type of pot used is important. The *gorshok* is made of clay, while the *chugun* is cast from iron; both are bulbous in shape. The pots are tightly covered to keep aromas and vitamins intact as the slow cooking imparts a well-rounded flavor that can't be attained by faster stovetop cooking. Porridges, soups, stews, and vegetables were all traditionally prepared in these vessels.

Various forms of slow cooking yield some of the most interesting dishes in the Russian repertoire. *Kundiumy,* dumplings that date from medieval times, are stuffed with dried mushrooms, buckwheat, and greens before being baked, rather than boiled. After they turn crisp, they are steamed in the oven in mushroom broth until they become soft and slightly chewy. Fish cakes are pan-fried, then steamed until moist and tender. The most classic form of Russian cabbage soup, *sutochnye shchi* (twenty-four-hour *shchi*) is made by slowly simmering beef bones in water to make a rich broth. Sauerkraut is stewed in the oven until it caramelizes before being added to the broth. This double slow cooking makes an exceedingly flavorful soup.

Baking, Roasting, Boiling, and Poaching

The masonry stove reaches a high internal temperature that is just right for baking breads and pies, placed directly on the hearth after the hot embers have been scraped to the back of the oven. Hearth baking yields a beautifully burnished crust. For those who could afford them, large cuts of meat were also roasted at high temperatures, though roasting is not the age-old practice that steaming is. Researchers trying to parse old recipes are frequently frustrated by the all-purpose Russian word *zharit',* whose English equivalents include roasting, frying, searing, grilling, and broiling. None of these cooking methods are characteristic of the most traditional Russian cuisine, since they don't take advantage of the masonry stove's greatest attributes and, except for roasting, they demand the cook's active involvement. Nevertheless, they gradually entered into Russian culinary practice.

Boiling, however, has long been used to make dumplings, as well as jam, whose name, *varen'e,* comes from the root "to boil" (*-var*). The same root yields the word *vzvar,* which in the past referred to a variety of different foods and drinks made by boiling. In its simplest form, *vzvar* was the Slavonic word for sauce, which was largely replaced in the eighteenth century by the French cognate *sous. Vzvar* also described what we would call a garnish for meats, usually made from strongly flavored vegetables like cabbage and onions, gently boiled with vinegar and honey for a sweet-and-sour taste; or from tart berries like cranberries or lingonberries. Finally, *vzvar* is an old word for a once-common drink made by boiling spices and dried fruits or berries with beer.

The most resonant association for the root "to boil" is found in the samovar, the urn for making tea whose name literally means "self-boiler." For Russians, tea making is serious business, and even if few people these days go to the trouble of heating water with charcoal or pinecones in an old-fashioned samovar, the hiss of the urn—still a ubiquitous trope in literature and cartoons—signals cheerful anticipation of hospitality to come. Russians use aural cues to know when the samovar is ready. As the water heats inside the brass urn, it reverberates, its sound changing as the temperature rises from a kind of unintelligible song to the whoosh of a wave coming to shore to the seething that indicates that the water has come to a boil.

FIGURE 5. William Carrick, Russian peasants at the samovar, 1860–69. William Carrick was a Scottish photographer who had a studio in Saint Petersburg, where he created an "Album of Russian Types" depicting regular people like peasants, street hawkers, and tradesmen. He printed the photographs in the newly discovered *carte de visite* format that was popular among collectors. This staged photograph shows muzhiks in typical dress drinking tea from saucers. The teapot atop the samovar holds *zavarka,* strongly brewed tea. Collection of the Kunstkamera, Saint Petersburg. © MAE RAN 2021.

Poaching foods in a small amount of liquid is more common in Russian haute cuisine. Poaching is favored for delicate foods like certain kinds of fish, which need to be cooked gently at a low temperature to retain their fine texture and flavor.

Frying

Pan-fried foods have their own specific name in Russian, *pria-zhenye,* to differentiate them from goods baked directly on the hearth without fat (*pudovye*). Pan-frying is used for small breads, certain pancakes, and various hand pies, often savory, that are fried in a generous amount of hot fat, but without being deep-fried, or immersed in fat (for which the term *zharit'* is usually used). Unlike pies baked in the oven, the dough for pan-fried pies is frequently prepared without yeast (*presnoe*). Meat and vegetable cutlets are also pan-fried. The fat used can be butter, vegetable oil, or a mixture of the two; on fast days, when animal fats were proscribed, vegetable oils like hempseed or flaxseed were de rigueur. After sunflower-seed oil was introduced in the eighteenth century, it became the vegetable oil of choice, although contemporary Russian cooks now also have access to olive oil.

Fermentation

A harsh climate and short growing season made it crucial to preserve summer's bounty for the long winter ahead, and preservation by fermentation is one of the hallmarks of Russian cuisine. The oldest Russian drinks were created through the fermentation of honey to produce mead, and black bread to yield kvass. And the secular trinity in Russia would have to be vodka, pickles, and rye bread, all three of which rely on fermentation for their deliciousness. Russian vodka is distilled from a fermented mash of grains like rye, barley, and hard winter wheat. Russian pickles have nothing to do with vinegar: they are the result of the lactic acid fermentation that occurs when cucumbers are layered with garlic and herbs in a salt brine (mushrooms treated the same way are another beloved Russian dish). The probiotic-rich pickle brine is famously used in some of Russia's most classic soups, and a potent Cossack-style mustard is made by mixing brown mustard seeds with brine instead of vinegar. The classic Russian rye bread is made with a sourdough starter to give it a wonderfully sour tang. Even fine wheat loaves were sometimes subjected to a very slow, anaerobic fermentation by wrapping the dough loosely in a towel and submerging it in a barrel full of cold water until the parcel rose to the top of the bowl, indicating that it was light enough to shape.

Related to fermentation (*kvashenie*) is brining (*mochenie*). While vegetables generally undergo lactic acid fermentation in a salty solution (such as dill pickles from cucumbers, sauerkraut from cabbage, beet kvass from beets), Russians preserve more delicate fruits by immersing them in weaker brine, containing only around 3.5 percent salt. Favored fruits for brining are apples—particularly the tart Antonovka variety—tomatoes, watermelon, and berries. The effect is not salty, but almost wine-like, and the longer the fruits are held in the brine, the more effervescent they become. On his deathbed, in January, Alexander Pushkin, Russia's national poet, called out for brined cloudberries.

Russia's beloved tea is also a product of fermentation. Although the Russians manufacture very little tea, they certainly drink it, and country dwellers gather fireweed leaves (familiarly known as "Ivan tea" [*Ivan-chai*]) to oxidize into green tea or ferment into black. The leaves contain copious amounts of Vitamin C and anti-inflammatory flavonoids and are a popular remedy for a variety of ills. In the past, shady merchants passed this tea off as genuine Chinese tea, which was far more costly.

Culturing

Another form of fermentation is culturing, which uses a bacterial starter culture to bring about the desired flavor and texture. Kombucha, made from tea, is one example of this process (though its starter also includes yeast). The Russians have enjoyed this drink for centuries. During the Soviet era, many families kept a three-liter jar of kombucha fermenting on their windowsills as a healthy, homegrown alternative to the carbonated soft drinks of the West that they could not obtain. But the real art of culturing in Russia is most visible in dairy products, whose flavors range from subtle to intense. *Tvorog* is farmer's cheese made by gently heating soured milk until curds form. *Prostokvasha,* whose name translates as "simply soured," is eaten as we eat yogurt. To make it, raw milk is allowed to sour and thicken naturally; a crust of sourdough rye added to the milk accelerates the process. *Varenets* is prepared from milk that has been slowly baked until its sugars caramelize, yielding an incomparably rich taste. *Riazhenka* is nearly identical but contains additional cream. And of course the Russian kitchen is unimaginable without *smetana,* or sour cream.

Sour cream was the basis for so-called Russian butter (*russkoe* or *toplyonoe maslo*), a type of clarified butter designed for long storage. When properly prepared, it could keep for years. The technique of heating butter was likely introduced from the Ottoman Empire, where clarified butter was used in cooking. Russians adapted the process. They melted butter with a rather large quantity of water, skimming the foam from the top, then let it settle before straining out the remaining solids. When firm, the butter was pierced to allow any remaining water to drain off. Only then was it packed into tubs to store in a cool cellar.

Despite its keeping properties, Russian butter could turn rancid when improperly stored. Because it was such an expensive product, people were loath to discard it. So it was reheated, sometimes two or three times, each time to the butter's detriment. Enter a better butter, known as *chukhonskoe,* a colloquial term meaning "Finnish." This type of butter was generally cultured and usually also made from sour cream (though high-quality sweet cream butter could sometimes be sold under this name). It was preserved by light salting and never heated. Cookbooks frequently specified Finnish butter in recipes for fine cooking.

Another cultured product is kefir, a slightly effervescent milk beverage. While the cultured milk products native to Russia are naturally fermented with lactobacilli, kefir is made with "grains," a combination of bacteria and yeast. The Nobel prize-winning scientist Ilya Metchnikoff promoted the benefits of kefir for longevity in pioneering studies during the early twentieth century, demonstrating the salubrious activity of what we now call probiotics in the gut. Initially introduced for medicinal purposes, kefir by the 1930s had become a Russian dairy standard and remains popular today.

Curing and Salting

Until the Stroganov family (of later beef Stroganoff fame) began extracting salt from the rich reserves in the Siberian north in the early sixteenth century, salt was a precious commodity that was used only sparingly. Unlike countries with more temperate climates, Russia did not have miles of coastline where salt could be evaporated with the help of the sun. The domestic extraction of salt relied on an ingenious but arduous method of cold-climate salt production that had been perfected along the shores of the White Sea in the Arctic. By the twelfth century, long before cast-iron evaporators came into use, the Indigenous Sami people had found ways to obtain salt from both seawater and from the saltwater marshes along the coast. They took advantage of winter's hard frosts to pour saltwater onto evergreen boughs. When the water evaporated in the cold, dry air, salt crystals naturally flavored with pine were left behind. This salt was very expensive and reserved for curing the best fish. The Sami also devised a process that involved cooling saltwater slowly to ensure that the ice that formed on top was nearly pure water, with the salt concentrated below in the brine. By repeatedly removing the layers of ice as they formed, the workers ended up with brine so high in salt that it crystallized when brought into the warmth of their tents. This freezing process was tricky, though, because if the water cooled too quickly, the salt compounds would be trapped within the ice, rather than settling into the unfrozen brine.

The White Sea salt works came to be closely identified with the magisterial Solovetsky Monastery, founded in 1436 on the Solovetsky Islands in the middle of the White Sea. These salt works were so lucrative that despite its remote location, the monastery became Russia's second wealthiest religious community. Besides selling their salt, the monks used it to preserve the fat herring they fished in late summer and fall. Layered in brine often flavored with coriander, this herring was so exquisite that barrelsful were sent straight to the table of the tsar. The monks sold the salt to the local Pomors, who turned out to be adept tradesmen. They carried it along the so-called salt highways leading from the North to central Russia and beyond. Pomorka salt (also called Morianka) was known as "white gold" and so prized that its export was discouraged.

The folktale "Salt" points to how precious salt once was. A ship captained by the beloved character Ivan the Fool is blown off course to a remote island, where Ivan discovers an enormous mountain consisting of "pure Russian salt." He loads the salt onto his ship and sails to a far-off land, where he hopes to engage in trade. But salt is unheard-of in that land, and when Ivan asks the king for permission to sell the salt, the king dismisses it as "white sand." Undeterred, Ivan goes into the kitchen. He asks to rest briefly and, when the royal cooks aren't looking, surreptitiously salts the food. At dinner the king declares the food the tastiest he has ever eaten. He summons the cooks to find out what they have done. Claiming no knowledge of any secret, they suggest that he summon the boy. So Ivan appears before the king. Fearing punishment, he cries: "I'm guilty, your Majesty! I seasoned all the dishes and sauces with Russian salt. That is what we do in my country." The king is so pleased that he rewards Ivan with gold and silver in equal measure to the salt.

With his annexation of Siberia, Ivan IV encouraged the exploitation of salt, thereby dramatically lowering its cost and, not incidentally, making the Stroganovs enormously wealthy. Later in the century the industry expanded into the salt-rich Astrakhan region to the south.

Near the mouth of the Caspian Sea, Astrakhan boasted another source of wealth: the magnificent sturgeon, whose roe was salted to turn into caviar. Caviar is nearly as synonymous with Russia as vodka, and the two make an ideal union. The Russians most likely learned to process fish eggs with salt from Greek traders along the Black Sea coast, but it wasn't until the Mongol occupation that a caviar industry developed in Astrakhan. The abundant salt in the Astrakhan region made it a logical place for a caviar industry to flourish. The Caspian Sea is home to several species of sturgeon, which Russians have long considered the king of fish. The beluga sturgeon can be monstrously large, weighing over two thousand pounds (though such specimens—and even the beluga itself—are rare today). Since a female sturgeon carries up to 15 percent of her weight in eggs, a single fish might yield three hundred pounds or

FIGURE 6. Lev Borodulin, *Anything for the People!,* 1960s. This image promising abundance and glorifying the food industry belies the reality of food shortages during the Soviet years. Because these tins of caviar are destined for export, the photograph's title carries more than a touch of irony. Collection of the Multimedia Art Museum, Moscow.

more of roe. Astonishing numbers of sturgeon were caught well into the eighteenth century as they swam up the Volga River to spawn—some accounts claim up to 250 giant belugas an hour.

Fish eggs are fragile and highly perishable. Salting not only helps to preserve the roe but also protects it from cold by lowering the temperature at which the eggs freeze. The egg sac is extracted by hand, and the roe is gently pushed through a sieve to separate it from the membrane before being mixed with brine. The best fresh caviar, which usually contains less than 3 percent salt, is known as *malossol.*

Caviar was once eaten very differently than it is today, as the German scribe Adam Olearius noted on his diplomatic voyage to Russia. From *The Travels of Olearius in Seventeenth-Century Russia* we learn that "they expel the roe from the membrane in which it is contained, salt it, and after it has stood for six to eight days, mix it with pepper and finely chopped onions. Some also add vinegar and country butter before serving it. It is not a bad dish. If one pours a bit of lemon juice over it, instead of vinegar, it gives a good appetite, and has a restorative effect."

Olearius had taken part in two voyages to Persia, beginning in 1633, both sponsored by Frederick III, Duke of Holstein-Gottorp. Frederick hoped to negotiate an overland trade route for silk, for which he also needed permission to travel through Muscovy. Although Olearius's praise of caviar may sound faint, he was in fact more open to local foodways than other early Western visitors to Russia—his disdain focused instead on Russian drunkenness, debauchery, and women's excessive use of makeup.

Medieval Russians often ate caviar hot. For the Muscovite dish *kal'ia,* pressed caviar was sliced into thin rounds, placed in an earthenware pot with chopped onion, black pepper, pickles, pickle brine, and water, then steamed in the oven of the masonry stove. Sometimes it was treated as we do shad roe, by sprinkling the whole egg sac with salt and pepper, dusting it with flour, and pan-frying it. A sauce made of onion, cranberry, or saffron was often served alongside. Still popular are quick caviar pancakes (*ikrianki*), for which the fish eggs are either stirred into the batter or beaten into it for a stronger taste. So abundant was caviar that in *A Gift to Young Housewives* the ever-practical Elena Molokhovets suggests substituting protein-rich pressed caviar for egg whites to clarify bouillon. To please richer palates, caviar was transported overland in linden wood barrels from the Caspian Sea to Moscow and Saint Petersburg. For the tsar and other extravagant consumers, live sturgeon were transported in carts or sleighs, and later in special railway cars equipped with fish tanks, so that the eggs could be harvested on site for optimal freshness. By the mid-nineteenth century, the finest sturgeon caviar had become rare enough that it was generally served unadorned, presented on toast points at fancy dinners.

As a result of pollution and poaching, all varieties of Caspian sturgeon are endangered today, and the spectacular beluga is nearly extinct. Russia is no longer the world's leading producer of caviar: that honor belongs to China, which fishes kaluga sturgeon in the Amur River, on the border with Russia. Russians continue to enjoy salted roe from salmon, burbot, pike, carp, grayling, and Arctic char, though sturgeon roe—especially when processed fresh and unpasteurized—remains the gold standard.

Freezing

Not surprisingly, Russians have long exploited the cold as a means of preservation, using their harsh environment to relative advantage. The wealthy maintained icehouses long before they were common in Europe, and monasteries kept their famous meads in ice cellars—cold cellars with ice pits. One specialty of the Russian North is *stroganina*, shaved frozen fish or sometimes venison. Fish is caught during the winter months, when it is at its fattiest, and hung outside to freeze. To serve, the fish is held vertically while paper-thin slices are shaved off with a sharp knife. The shavings are often dipped in flavored salts, and they literally melt in your mouth.

Saint Petersburg was home to a storied winter meat market. Deep drifts of snow had whole and half carcasses of cows, pigs, and sheep planted upright in them, legs thrust high into the air as if frozen in some strange ballet. Thanks to the frigid temperatures, animals could be put on display right after slaughter, their shapes looming stiff and dark against the white snow. Colorfully dressed hawkers sold smaller cuts of meat from their sleds, and shoppers could choose from an astonishing variety of fats—from beef, pork, and sheep to walrus and bear—in shades ranging from white to cream and yellow. Buyers had to beware the unscrupulous vendors who artificially inflated the carcasses by blowing air into them, thereby also inflating the prices.

In modern times, apartment dwellers with little indoor storage space take advantage of cold temperatures to keep *pel'meni* (Siberian dumplings) and vodka at the ready. Prepared but uncooked dumplings are hung outdoors in winter from a windowsill or balcony, ready to be hauled inside at a moment's notice and dropped into a pot of boiling water. Vodka, whose high alcohol content keeps it from freezing solid, is also kept on a cold windowsill to maintain a perfect drinking temperature.

Drying

Mushrooms, berries, fish, and vegetables are all dried both to preserve them for storage and to intensify their flavors. Fresh mushroom soup, for instance, is subtle, but when mushrooms are dried and reconstituted in water, they yield a more richly flavored broth, excellent when paired with hearty grains like barley. Similarly, dried fruits baked into a pie or roasted with meat add depth of flavor. Drying also makes it possible to enjoy fruit compotes all year round. When dried, small freshwater fish like vendace, roach, and smelts become the perfect salty accompaniment to beer. Even sauerkraut was frequently dried in the past, both to make a different version of Russia's classic cabbage soup, *shchi*, and to serve as dry rations for travelers and for the navy, since it helped prevent scurvy during long sea voyages.

Dietary Dictates

Historically, Russians have had remarkably little agency in determining what they eat. Survival has depended on forces beyond their control. For early farmers, the vagaries of climate made each year's harvest unpredictable, generating uncertainty about whether a family would eat well or starve. When the Russian Orthodox church gained power, it exerted control not only over people's religious life but also their diet by dividing the year into fast (*postnyi*) days and feast (*skoromnyi*) days that largely coincided with the agricultural calendar. Most peasants adhered to the strict regimen that dictated exactly what they could and could not eat on any given day. The nobility, with access to a greater variety of foods, followed these dicta less rigorously and were no doubt pleased when the church, after lengthy debate, determined that caviar could be consumed on all but the most stringent fast days. Tsarist edicts also exerted dietary control, limiting or promoting access to vodka, mandating consumption of ocean (not just freshwater) fish, and enforcing cultivation of the once-suspect potato.

Integrating the potato into the Russian diet was no easy process. Peter the Great had first encountered potatoes when visiting Amsterdam in 1697. He shipped a sack to Count Boris Sheremetev, with the request that Sheremetev promote them in Russia. Nothing seems to have come of this initiative, however, and the potato gambit languished until 1765, when a senate resolution encouraged their cultivation. But peasants were wary of this new vegetable, especially the religious sect of Old Believers, who were convinced that because the tuber grows underground and has "eyes," it was the devil's fruit.

Potatoes gradually entered into cultivation, but as late as 1840 they were still not fully accepted and were largely considered famine food. A series of poor grain harvests led to several ukases commanding potato cultivation. The peasants believed that these decrees were auguries of the Apocalypse and the imminent arrival of the Antichrist. So they revolted, in what came to be known as the "potato riots." In several instances the army had to be called in, and numerous peasants were killed. Only after the most violent of these protests, in 1842, did the government choose a gentler form of persuasion in the form of propaganda, and within two decades potatoes had become a common crop.

There was some merit to the peasants' resistance, however. Though rye is far more labor-intensive than potatoes to cultivate and has to be processed into flour to make bread, it is also far richer in protein, fiber, fats, and carbohydrates, as well as most vitamins and minerals. Potatoes proved a reliable and important source of calories, but as a primary source of nutrients—and as a touchstone of Russian identity—rye was superior.

One criticism that could never be leveled against the potato was that it is a patrician food. Thus potatoes, the staple of the masses, not only survived but thrived during Soviet times, often in the form of pan-fried potato "cutlets" as a meat replacement. Meanwhile, the Soviets anathematized other foods, like chocolate, as too bourgeois, and dietitians such as Manuil Pevzner advocated for a proletarian diet based on "calm" foods that wouldn't agitate the system. The project to create a new, transformative Soviet way of life was energetically taken up by the state food-service organization, Narpit, which in 1928 sent a book of directives to every cafeteria in the country. Condemning the names of many dishes as aristocratic, foreign, or bourgeois, the book provided lists of appropriately proletarian replacements. For instance, Nikolaevsky *shchi*, named in honor of the tsar, became simply "*shchi* made from chopped cabbage," while crème du Barry turned into "creamed cauliflower soup." Béchamel was rather unappetizingly transformed into "white thick milk sauce," and sturgeon *américaine* into "sturgeon in tomato sauce." The Narpit mandate erased the names of hundreds of well-known dishes and caused knowledge of them to disappear for subsequent generations.

In the 1930s, as part of his campaign to make life "more joyous," Stalin did an about-face and encouraged the mass production of such luxury items as chocolate, ice cream, and champagne. Meanwhile, meat, always an object of desire, remained expensive and hard to obtain. Systems of food distribution—whether through official channels, private bartering, or the black market—ultimately determined how well each family ate. Special emphasis was placed on children's nutrition: generations of kids grew up on daily porridges of farina (cream of wheat), buckwheat, or oatmeal (whose brand name Hercules screamed nutrition and became synonymous with rolled oats).

Despite these shifting dietary prescriptions and proscriptions, Russians retain a strong sense of what constitutes "real food." The Russian language uses two very different words for food. Food in general (which can also be a meal) is *eda*. But then there is *pishcha*, food that can be elevated to metaphor (food for thought, food for the soul, food of the gods) while simultaneously indicating something absolutely basic and essential. Sourdough rye bread, for instance, is *pishcha*; white bread is not. Lacto-fermented sauerkraut is *pishcha*; cucumber pickles, though a beloved accompaniment to vodka or a meal, are not. The distinction might seem subtle, but it actually speaks to survival. Tellingly, the adage "Cabbage soup and kasha, that's our food" uses the word *pishcha,* and not merely for its sibilant effect.

Russian ideas about healthy eating reflect the dietary demands of a cold climate and favor substantial foods that keep well, and are rich in fiber, nutrients, and vitamins. When Russian peasants first encountered lettuce around the time of Peter the Great, they laughed at the foreigners who had introduced it and at the grandees who enjoyed what to them seemed like grass—it was not real food. Even after it became a fairly common garden crop, lettuce (called simply *salat* or "salad") never won the peasants' hearts. Only after the collapse of the Soviet Union did it finally find a regular place at the Russian table. People also laughed at the early-twentieth-century vegetarian proselytizer Natalia Nordman-Severova, who advocated a diet of wild plants and hay as a means of eradicating widespread hunger. In her 1911 *Cookbook for the Hungry* (*Povaryonnaia kniga dlia golodaiushchikh*) she insisted that a Russian meadow provided a solution. For a quick and tasty meal, one need only go out into the summertime fields and pick fresh plants like lady's mantle, goutweed, angelica, mountain sorrel, yarrow, timothy grass, and canary grass, then sauté them with celery, parsley, dill, and onion in a little olive oil. For winter, she recommended drying the grasses and tying them in cheesecloth to make an instant bouillon. In summer, she was known to serve a soup of freshly mown meadow hay to Saint Petersburg's artistic elite when they came to the Wednesday salons she hosted with her partner, the Realist painter Ilya Repin, at their elegant dacha on the Gulf of Finland. To her great frustration, Nordman never managed to convert Repin to vegetarianism.

Even though Nordman's diet was dismissed as not substantial enough to constitute real food, its kinship to traditional folk medicine and insistence upon good health reflect another constant in Russian dietary practices, one that continues to this day: a domestic approach to illness and the belief in the curative power of herbs. Although this folk knowledge arose long ago in villages that lacked a clinic or even a doctor, herbal wisdom is still commonly shared and passed down through generations. Herbs, both fresh and dried, are used not only to flavor vodka but also to make tisanes to calm the nervous system, soothe upset stomachs and aching muscles, increase appetite, boost immunity, and encourage sleep. The leaves, roots, and berries of plants like raspberries and blackcurrants, mint and lemon balm, St. John's wort, and rhodiola are gathered and mixed into herbal blends.

Among the peasantry, fat, preferably lard, was valued more than the protein in meat. Soups were judged by the amount of fat glistening on the surface, and fatty fish, along with their livers (which we now know to be rich in omega-3 fatty acids), were highly prized. Equally important was the tang produced by lactic acid fermentation. According to the nineteenth-century chemist Alexander Engelgardt, who chronicled his observations of peasant life, a sour taste was the most crucial property in food. Without the acidic element, he wrote, "dinner was not dinner for the working man." Engelgardt went so far as to claim that for the laborers on his country estate, worm-ridden sauerkraut was preferable to none at all, because they so enjoyed the sour taste and believed in its attendant nutritive properties. If for some reason sauerkraut or beet kvass wasn't available as a souring agent in soup, the peasants added whey, buttermilk, or pickle brine to achieve the desired taste.

Based on a strange case he encountered in 1838, a certain Doctor Figurin concluded that the benefits of fermented foods are both psychological and physical. Reporting in the medical journal *The Friend of Health,* he described the treatment of an otherwise healthy forty-year-old woman who was admitted to a Saint Petersburg hospital in the grip of a madness so violent that she had to be restrained in a straitjacket and tied with sheets to the hospital bed. Her mental anguish was accompanied by severe gastric distress that caused incessant vomiting. Spanish fly (crushed, dried blister beetles), among other interventions, eventually alleviated the madness, but the gastric problems persisted. The patient begged the doctor for "something sour" instead of the laudanum he was treating her with, so he began feeding her spoonsful of sauerkraut, which she accepted "with delight." Within twenty-four hours her vomiting had stopped, and after two days the doctor discontinued the sauerkraut regimen. At this point the patient's appetite had returned, and she requested sour cabbage soup with black bread. On a diet of this food (*pishcha*), she soon returned to normal and was sent home.

After the 1917 Russian Revolution, the state sought to institute new norms for healthy eating, establishing the Scientific Research Institute for the Physiology of Nutrition as early as 1920. In the classic Soviet cookbook *The Book of Tasty and Healthy Food*, first published in 1939 under Stalin's direction, a section called "The Meaning of Rational Eating for the Individual" immediately follows the introduction, laying out the importance of proteins, fats, carbohydrates, vitamins, and minerals in the diet. In later editions this section became "The Foundations of Rational Eating" and "Nutrition and Health," and by 1978 it had grown from the original two pages to twenty-three, detailing in numerous charts the bases of a healthy diet from a scientific perspective. Inevitably, much of this advice, like the recipes that followed, was aspirational, since obtaining vitamin-rich foods like fresh citrus was often impossible. Yet despite the overall monotony of comestibles in the Soviet era, people never disdained the highly nutritious foods of the traditional Russian diet, such as sourdough rye bread, buckwheat porridge, whole grains, lacto-fermented vegetables, and honey.

After the collapse of the Soviet Union, the country was flooded with Western foods, offering a previously unheard-of bounty of citrus fruits, bananas, kiwifruit, and grapes. People clamored for the new, even in the form of less wholesome baguettes made of wheat or fast foods from the likes of McDonald's and Pizza Hut. Trends in fashion also brought new problems to Russian society, as girls and young women sought to emulate the stick-thin models they saw in advertising. Indeed, the "grass" that their forebears had once disdained became the focus of their diet, in the form of salad.

Meals and Mealtimes

Mealtimes in Russia varied according to social class. Peasants working in the field rose before dawn for an early breakfast, then took breaks in the field at mid-morning and noon, when they ate dinner (*obed*), the main meal of the day. The evening meal was lighter and taken at home, except during harvest times, when work continued nearly nonstop. The more leisured classes rose later, beginning the day with a light breakfast, followed by a late-morning snack. Dinner was served at around two o'clock, though it could be enjoyed at any time between noon and three. Late afternoon was punctuated by a snack called *poldnik,* to tide people over until supper (*uzhin*) at eight or nine in the evening, sometimes followed by tea. A late-night snack often rounded out the day.

The defining element of dinner was, for all social classes, a bowl of soup, served either with black bread or another carbohydrate-rich accompaniment. For the peasantry, soup *was* the meal, but wealthy diners enjoyed multiple courses. The most distinctive aspect of Russian dining, and one that often takes the uninitiated by surprise, is the first course, known as *zakuska* (appetizer). In tsarist times, wealthy homes boasted a separate *zakuska* table, and often even a separate room where the appetizers (*zakuski*) were served. This practice of providing a buffet of foods that could remain set out for hours without spoiling took hold in the eighteenth century, though the concept of small bites had existed long before. (In Vladimir Dal's magisterial dictionary of the Russian language, *zakuska* is defined as "vodka with pickles and other foods.") The fashion for *zakuski* was especially well suited to the habits of Russian gentry on their country estates. Because visitors had to deal with bad roads and unpredictable weather, they would frequently arrive late, and famished. With a *zakuska* table awaiting them, guests could refresh themselves immediately on arrival. The rise of restaurants in the early nineteenth century made these formal *zakuska* tables available to the urban public.

Eating Out

Street food has long been a vital, and vivid, aspect of Russian urban life. Vendors plied the streets, hawking specialties like *sbiten'* (a hot, spiced honey drink sold in urns carried like backpacks), hot *pirozhki* (small hand pies), the Moscow *kalach* (a purse-shaped loaf of bread made from the finest wheat flour), and *kisel'* (a hearty pudding of oatmeal or dried peas). In addition, stalls were set up in the famous outdoor "rows" of Moscow and Saint Petersburg, where people could buy food to take away or sit down at long tables to have a quick bite. The tradition of street food, unlike other attributes of prerevolutionary life that were summarily eradicated, thrived throughout the Soviet period, with stands selling blini, *ponchiki* (doughnuts), and *chebureki,* Crimean meat pies. Many of the kiosks selling these foods were erected outside train and subway stations. The post-Soviet years saw greater government regulation and homogenization of these kiosks, as fast-food chains like Kroshka-Kartoshka (for stuffed baked potatoes) and Teremok (for traditional Russian fare) gained a foothold.

More substantial eating—and mainly drinking—establishments existed as early as the eleventh century. The first was the *korchma,* a type of tavern. Patrons drank mead, kvass, and beer brewed without hops, usually bringing a bite from home to accompany the drinks. The atmosphere was club-like, with a large hall for socializing or discussing civic affairs. This form of gathering was greatly curtailed by an 1150 edict decreeing that *korchmy* henceforward had to pay duties to the ruling princes. Eventually their ownership was regulated and government taxes were imposed; they subsequently declined in popularity.

A different kind of tavern, the *kabak,* came into being by order of Ivan IV. He initially established these facilities for the sole benefit of his elite guards, though they were later opened up to different social groups. Because the *kabaki* were heavily taxed, they were lucrative, and it was in the interest of the government to regulate them closely. These taverns could not sell food, only drink, especially the newly popular vodka (then known as *zeleno vino,* wine made from grain).

The next level of public dining in Russia developed under Peter the Great, with the establishment of the *traktir,* a tavern where food could be enjoyed along with alcohol, thus mitigating its effects—at least in theory. These places generally attracted a more refined clientele than the *kabaki* and eventually became known for their menus of traditional Russian food. Workers and other low-wage earners could grab a meal for a few kopecks at the *obzhornye riady* (glutton's rows)—colorful market food stalls that imaginatively repurposed leftovers into inexpensive pies—or at the grub houses known as *kharchevni.* A notch up from these grub houses were the affordable *kukhmisterskie* (from the German *Küchenmeister,* or chef) that arose at this time mainly to accommodate workers and students, many of whom lived in rooming houses or dormitories without kitchens. The *kukhmisterskie* offered the appealing option of takeout. At the opposite end of the spectrum were the coffeehouses that served a largely foreign clientele, especially in Saint Petersburg, and the elite private gentlemen's clubs that offered good food and camaraderie in elegantly furnished rooms.

Moscow's English Club, in particular, was renowned for its set menus, featuring both Russian and French dishes. Food consumption was as class-based in urban settings as in rural ones, just more complicated.

The first formal restaurants in Russia opened in the early nineteenth century, the very first in Saint Petersburg's Hotel du Nord (which today houses a popular bakery called Du Nord 1834). Coffeehouses began to be replaced by cafés where patrons could enjoy pastries and chocolate with their coffee, in addition to wine and more substantial fare. Throughout the nineteenth century, the government issued laws regulating the various types of eating establishments, many of them designed to keep Russia's rapidly changing social classes confined to the places they had historically frequented. By the century's end, the simple *kukhmisterskie* had been supplanted by the *stolovaia,* an institution that thrived in the Soviet era and lives on in Russia today. These inexpensive cafeterias varied in quality from abominable to excellent. Among the best were those organized in the early twentieth century by Russia's various vegetarian societies, which developed a reputation for good, fresh food and were frequented by surprisingly large numbers of people. In 1916, in the midst of World War I, the two cafeterias sponsored by the Kiev Vegetarian Society provided over fifty thousand dinners.

After the revolution, workers increasingly ate at workplace canteens, set up as part of a major political effort to liberate women from domestic chores. Early propaganda posters proclaimed, "Down with kitchen slavery!" Meanwhile, visionary architects of the 1920s built "living cells"—one-room apartments whose only "kitchen" was a hot plate. Proper meals were to be taken with other residents of the apartment block in a large, communal facility. To

FIGURE 7. Arkady Shaikhet, *Factory Kitchen*, 1930. The Moscow truck factory that came to be known as the Likhachev factory boasted a model factory kitchen that served as the workers' canteen. The enormous room displays banners with rousing slogans, such as Lenin's creed "Study, study, study" and Stalin's exhortation to "fulfill in ten years what previously took one hundred years, lest the USSR be crushed." The building was demolished in 2016 to make way for a housing complex. Collection of the Multimedia Art Museum, Moscow.

supply the canteens, huge "factory kitchens" were designed by such leading Constructivists as Alexander Rodchenko. Predictably, because most of the staff were women, their "liberation" actually entailed much more grueling labor as they prepared and served food to a hundred people at a time before going home to face their own domestic chores.

Although enforced communal dining died out in the 1930s, workers' canteens and public cafeterias survived, on different terms. A system of state standards (GOST) was introduced in 1940, mandating that each dish in every canteen and cafeteria throughout the vast Soviet Union was to be prepared in precisely the same fashion, down to the last gram of all the ingredients, which themselves were categorized according to quality—an example of centralized planning taken to extremes. Thus, in theory, a Muscovite stopping for lunch at a cafeteria in Tashkent or Tallinn could expect to find *kotlety* (meat patties) that tasted exactly like those served at her local cafeteria. Although in practice cooks' abilities were reflected in the dishes they served, the GOST regulations succeeded in imposing a universal Soviet cuisine in the public sphere. Many of these Soviet dishes have become sentimental favorites today, as evidenced by the popularity of such recent cookbooks as Irina Chadeeva's *Baking by GOST: The Taste of Our Childhood*.

Of course, not everyone frequented cafeterias. Soviet citizens who held prestigious positions (scientists, writers, composers, and so on) were rewarded weekly with special "dry rations" that often included hard-to-obtain "deficit" items like caviar. And privileged quasi-private establishments boasted excellent dining rooms, like the one at the Writer's Union described in Mikhail Bulgakov's novel *The Master and Margarita,* where diners could feast on truffled thrush, woodcock, or sterlet served in a silver chafing dish—as long as their work remained acceptable to the Stalinist state.

As for public restaurants, Moscow, as recently as the early 1980s, had only two outstanding ones for its entire population of nine million, and neither specialized in Russian food. Aragvi featured Georgian cuisine, while Uzbekistan served up pilaf (*plov*) and kebabs. Both restaurants were effectively off-limits for most Soviet citizens—not only because they were too expensive, but because getting in required *blat*—"pull" or influence. Despite the standard line that the restaurant had no seats available, foreigners could often gain entry by slipping the doorman a pack of Marlboros or presenting a passport with a hard-currency bribe inside. Ordinary Russians accepted the circumstances and celebrated occasions like birthdays and weddings at large restaurants cum banquet halls, where dishes like chicken Kiev and Pozharsky cutlets were served to blaring music from a crooner onstage.

But even in Soviet times there existed plenty of casual eating spots, each of which specialized in a specific, beloved food: *pel'meni* (dumplings), blini, *chebureki, shashlyk* (meat kebabs), tea and pastries, and beer. For a truly quick bite there were *zakusochnye,* snack bars where you could wolf your food down while standing at high, round tables. For a quick refresher, it was always possible to guzzle a glass of kvass from one of the many bright yellow tanker trucks parked on street corners and squares.

Fast-food restaurants appeared in Russia at the very end of the Soviet era. McDonald's opened an outlet in Moscow in 1990 in a symbolic location on Pushkin Square, a mere twenty-minute walk from the Kremlin. Thousands of people stood for hours in line to be among the very first to try an American-style hamburger. Other foreign, and then Russian, fast-food outlets soon followed. Today, dining options are manifold. It is notable that some of Russia's trendiest restaurants reveal a return to traditional (or idealized traditional) fare, where diners can taste a re-creation of medieval Moscow's *kalach* or a bowl of hempseed porridge steamed with birch juice in a masonry stove.

2 *Hardship and Hunger*

Thickly sliced crusts, toasted on the outside and left moist on the inside, went especially well with tea. If you left the bread in the frying pan and ate it with a knife and fork—then you had a meal.

LIDIYA GINZBURG, *Blockade Diary*

On the evening of August 4, 2015, many viewers of the nightly news on Russia's state television channel were horrified to see food—literally tons of food—being destroyed at Russia's borders, from Kazakhstan to Belarus. Vladimir Putin had just decreed that meat, cheese, and vegetables imported from the EU and other Western nations were to be incinerated by "mobile crematoria"—an edict in response to the sanctions imposed a year earlier, after Russia invaded and annexed Crimea. The *Guardian* described the newscast: "'An operation to liquidate dozens of tons of contraband pork has taken place,' a news anchor announced . . . , followed by footage of triumphant customs officials apparently unveiling a huge consignment of 'Ukrainian' pork fat that was actually a Danish product with fake labels. Around 35 tonnes of pork, in blue containers, was thrown into incinerators." For Russians, this wanton destruction of food was hard to stomach. Over five hundred thousand people signed a petition requesting that the contraband foods be distributed to organizations and individuals in need. The request was denied.

Hunger, and all too frequently famine, has defined Russian history from its very beginnings. Except for the rich black-earth belt of chernozem of the steppe (a mere 8.7 percent of the country's total acreage), Russia's soil is mostly poor, and the growing season is quite short. Annual yield was historically limited by the conservative agricultural practices of the peasants, who adhered to a three-field system of crop rotation in which one-third of the land always lay unproductively fallow. The peasants' sowing practices were also outdated, as the crude wooden ploughs they used barely penetrated the soil. In each village, agricultural work was regulated by the mir, a self-governing body that controlled access to arable land and forests. In most villages, residents agreed to grow the same crops so that the harvest could be carried out communally. This system generally enabled the peasants to get by, as opposed to getting wealthy, although a small percentage, known as kulaks, became relatively prosperous. Agricultural reforms introduced in the late nineteenth century proved only marginally successful, and three-field rotation persisted until the forcible industrialization of agriculture under Stalin in the 1930s.

The earliest recorded histories of Russia, which chronicle events dating back to the year 852, tell of severe famines. Some descriptions are gruesome, like the one of the famine in Rostov in 1071, less than a hundred years after Russia had accepted Christianity. Intent on subverting the new religion, pagan priests accused distinguished women of causing the food shortages. As the *Primary Chronicle* relates, when the local women were brought to them, the priests, "by means of magic, stabbed each of the women in the back and drew out from their bodies wheat or fish. And they thus killed many women and took what they had for themselves." But of course the real factors behind this and Russia's subsequent periodic famines were environmental, including adverse weather and pests.

Chaff Bread and Begging for Crusts

In modern times, lack of government planning and relief assistance exacerbated the devastation caused by nature. The immediate cause of the dire famine that hit the Volga River region in 1891 was that year's poor harvest, but it was compounded by the government's failure to set up adequate systems of food distribution following the emancipation of the serfs thirty years earlier. To make matters worse, because grain was an important source of state revenue, the government continued to export it, thereby depleting reserves. That winter proved to be exceptionally bitter. People survived by gathering orach and acorns and cut the bitter, tannic inner bark (*zabolon'*) from birch trees, which was boiled until soft, then dried and ground into flour. This famine food was even worse than the chaff (*pushnoi*) bread the peasants regularly subsisted on when they had used up their stores. As Alexander Engelgardt described in his *Letters from the Country 1872–1887*, this bread was "made from unwinnowed rye, that is, a mixture of rye and chaff, [and was] milled directly into flour, from which bread is made in the usual way. This bread is a doughy mass filled with fine needles of chaff; it tastes all right, like ordinary bread, and it's less nutritious, but its main disadvantage is that it is hard to swallow, and anyone unaccustomed to it won't be able to swallow it at all. If he does manage to swallow it, then he'll start hawking and experience some kind of uncomfortable sensation in his mouth."

During normal hard times, the peasants had a built-in safety net. In the Russian countryside, the charitable sharing of bread was ritualized in the practice of "begging for crusts," which generally occurred in the winter or early spring when supplies of grain had run out. Children and elderly men and women (and, in the worst years, younger, able-bodied ones as well) would sling a sack over their shoulders and set out on foot or in carts for neighboring villages where food was more abundant to ask for small pieces of bread—sometimes only three inches square—from families who could spare some. A subtle etiquette developed for this practice, which was quite distinct from simply asking for a hand-out. People shared an unspoken sense of communal responsibility: Russian peasants knew that it was better for the hungry to maintain some dignity and not have to plead, since roles could easily reverse from year to year. If a family had only a single loaf of bread left, they would nevertheless give some to any person who came asking, then perhaps set out themselves to request help from others who might still have bread remaining. If they received more than they needed, they dried the extra bread in their stoves, to turn into rusks for hungry days ahead or to hand out to others in need.

Begging for crusts was accepted as part of the natural order, unlike simple begging, which was looked down upon. Anton Chekhov's short story "Oysters" (1884) is told from the point of view of a young boy whose father has been reduced to begging for spare change on the Moscow streets. The boy is overcome by "a strange illness" that makes him so weak that his legs buckle, his words get stuck in his throat, and his head lists to the side. He feels as though he's about to faint. "If I had landed in a hospital then, the doctors would have had to write on my chart: *Fames*—an illness that isn't in the medical textbooks." By the end of the story, the father's humiliation is so great that he goes mad, in part from his own lack of sustenance but also from shame.

Fatalism and the Russian Orthodox Church

During the Volga famine, Charles Emory Smith, the US minister to Saint Petersburg, published an essay on the crisis in the *North American Review,* ending with thoughts on what he called the peasantry's "stoicism": "Worn and emaciated with long struggle, and stripped of their material, the peasants face the requirements of a new harvest year under a load which would crush almost any other people. But their patience and endurance are without limit, and whatever their destiny, they accept it with a grim stoicism." Such endurance is more properly understood as fatalism, which for the Russian peasants arose out of circumstance in concert with a deep religious belief. As the Russian Orthodox church gained power, saints superseded the powerful pagan gods, but many folk beliefs were transmuted into superstition. Feared above all was the *ovinnik* who lived in the drying barn, which could easily catch fire. His anger could be forestalled by an offering of pies. If crops failed or livestock fell ill, the family might have displeased the grass-haired *polevik,* a spirit whose domain was the fields. Most frequently placated was the *domovoi,* the house spirit that lived beneath or behind the stove and was prone to mischief. He could be appeased with a portion of kasha or bread and salt. When a family moved into a new cottage, they were careful to carry a clay pot filled with coals from the old oven to ensure that the *domovoi* was comfortably established in his new home.

Through these beliefs and practices the peasants relinquished some responsibility for their lives—whether to a pagan god, a folk spirit, or a master who literally held them in thrall—thereby finding meaning in hardship. Christianity offered the most powerful seduction of all, an almighty God who ordained how their lives would proceed and whose word was transmitted through the Russian Orthodox church. In seeking to wean the peasantry from superstition and pagan beliefs (in which it only partially succeeded), the church found a tactical way to impose its strictures by codifying the annual patterns of hunger that most Russians experienced.

Nearly two hundred days of the year were designated as fast days, on which the consumption of meat and dairy products was restricted. Foodstuffs were divided into five categories: meat, dairy, fish, farinaceous, and vegetable. Russians observed meatless Wednesdays and Fridays; the most pious chose "to Monday" by avoiding forbidden foods on Mondays as well. These weekly fast days were supplemented by extended fasts, the most important of which was the great Lenten fast (forty days, plus the Passion week preceding Easter). Late winter coincided with the period of greatest hunger before the new crop of grain could be sown and the first shoots of wild greens appeared in the spring. There were also the Christmas or Filippov fast (six weeks preceding Christmas), the fast of Saints Peter and Paul (beginning in late May or June and lasting from one to six weeks, depending on when Easter fell); and the fast of the Dormition (two weeks in August). On the most stringent fast days (during Lent and the Dormition), even fish and vegetable oils were forbidden. In general, the poorer the household, the more strictly the inhabitants adhered to the fast, equating paucity with piety. Thus the Russian peasant diet consisted largely of what we would today consider vegan fare. As for the wealthy, fasting didn't necessarily entail deprivation. A mid-seventeenth-century state dinner held on a fast day included some five hundred dishes, not one made with meat products.

One common fast-day dish was *kulaga,* a nutritious, lightly fermented porridge of rye malt and rye flour that was prepared in the stove. But the real workhorse of the peasant kitchen, especially on fast days, was *gorokh*—dried peas, which were so ubiquitous that the idiom "in days of yore" is expressed in Russian as "in the time of Tsar Pea." Pease porridge, a type of *kisel,'* could turn into a delicacy or a disaster. Flour milled from the dried peas was boiled with water and seasoned with hempseed oil (although, if it wasn't a fast day, butter tasted much better, and the addition of garlic further elevated the porridge). This porridge was often served chilled, cut into squares, or used as a filling for savory pies. Some cooks even prepared "pea cheese" by mixing boiled peas with sourdough starter and a little vegetable oil and leaving the mixture to age for a couple of days. Dried green peas from the southern city of Rostov, famous for their sweetness and excellent texture, commanded a higher price than the more common yellow peas. But in the late nineteenth century unscrupulous vendors colored yellow peas with highly toxic Paris green compound, which led to widespread poisoning. This caused the price of the fine green peas to drop, and they ultimately disappeared from the market.

The Famine of 1921–1922

As dire as the 1891 famine was, the famine of 1921–22 was the worst recorded in Europe in modern times, according to a 1922 report by the League of Nations. Some thirty million people were threatened with starvation, and many engaged in desperate acts like eating the thatch from their cottage roofs. In isolated cases, people even stooped to cannibalism and necrophagy. The Russian words for these practices, *liudoedstvo* and *trupoedstvo*—literally "eating people" and "eating corpses"—are directly abhorrent, unlike the English terms, which feel abstracted thanks to their Spanish and Greek roots. Like earlier Russian famines, this catastrophe was brought on by two years of severe drought, but it was many times magnified by the consecutive cataclysms of World War I, the Russian Revolution, and the Civil War, as well as by Lenin's demand that the peasants hand over their grain to the state. Five million people died of starvation or famine-related disease.

Because the new Soviet state had no food reserves, it was forced to request aid from abroad. The writer Maxim Gorky interceded to negotiate help from the US secretary of commerce, Herbert Hoover. In 1919 Hoover had founded the American Relief Administration to aid Europe after the ravages of World War I, and now he made the politically difficult decision to send significant aid to the Bolshevik state. The American relief workers were initially enthusiastic about their mission to a seemingly exotic land, but their sense of high adventure was soon dispelled by the horrors they witnessed. The great Russian poet Velimir Khlebnikov described these horrors in his 1921 poem "Hunger" (here in Paul Schmidt's translation):

> Roast mouse.
> Their son fixed it, went and caught them in the field.
> They lie stretched out on the table,
> their long dark tails.

Today it's a decent dinner,
a real good meal!
Just a while back the housewife would shudder
and holler, smash the pitcher to smithereens
if she found a mouse drowned in the cream.

Because Russia's rail network had been destroyed in the war, the American relief workers had to improvise. They organized enormous caravans of camels from Central Asia, which could withstand the harsh winter weather, to transport nonperishable foodstuffs to the starving people. The American Relief Administration eventually contributed over fifty million dollars and saved over ten million lives through their soup kitchens and food transports to remote regions.

Collectivization

After seven years of war and revolution, the Russian economy was in a shambles, so in 1921 Lenin introduced the New Economic Policy (NEP), under which limited capitalist activities were allowed. Initially state policy encouraged the individual enterprise of the prosperous peasants known as kulaks, but by the end of the decade the Soviet government had turned against them. Any peasant who appeared relatively well off or who used hired hands on his farm could be labeled an enemy of the people, a counterrevolutionary, or a speculator in grain. In 1929 Stalin announced the Communist Party's intention to "liquidate the kulak as a class" as part of a brutal campaign to collectivize agriculture—to turn privately owned farms into large state holdings. The "cleansing" activity reached its height in 1932 and 1933 in Ukraine, the breadbasket of the Soviet Union. Millions of kulaks were arrested and executed, sent to labor camps, or deported to remote regions of Siberia and Central Asia. Their property was confiscated. The poorer peasants who remained were not spared either. Their livestock, grain, and other foodstuffs were requisitioned. Some of the seized food was intended for distribution in Moscow, but all too often the grain was simply dumped into huge piles, where it rotted. These piles were guarded day and night to ensure that no one could take any grain, even though people were dying of starvation. Red Army soldiers and volunteers went from house to house searching cellars and barns to uncover any food the peasants might have stashed away. Thus began the horrifying, state-sponsored famine in Ukraine known as the Holodomor. Not only did it kill nearly four million people, but it also effectively destroyed the region's productive agriculture.

In its drive to mechanize agriculture, the government created two types of farms. Collective farms (*kolkhozy*) were consolidated from what had been small, privately held plots of land, while state farms (*sovkhozy*) were established on larger, formerly landed estates. Moscow directed a centrally planned economy that determined allocations of seed, livestock, and equipment and dictated often-unattainable yields. Although some collective farms raised livestock, meat was in short supply throughout the Soviet years, since roughly half the existing livestock had perished during collectivization, either slaughtered by the peasants or lost to famine. The Soviet meat industry never fully recovered. Adding to the dire situation was Stalin's promotion of the biologist Trofim Lysenko's theories of plant evolution, which proved disastrous to Soviet agriculture. In a complete abandonment of the laws of genetics, Lysenko claimed that in the right environment, plants could acquire beneficial new traits that would then be passed on, in

FIGURE 8. Max Alpert, *Seizing Grain from Kulaks*, November 1, 1930. As part of Stalin's program of collectivization, members of the Komsomol—the Young Communist League—confiscate grain that someone had hidden in a cemetery. Confiscated grain was transported to distribution points and kept under guard. But the grain was often left to rot, even as millions of people starved. Sputnik Images.

Marxist fashion, to the next generation. He froze the seeds of winter wheat and rye and sowed them in the spring instead of the fall, insisting that this practice, called vernalization, would not only increase yields multifold, but would also allow agriculture to be practiced more widely in the USSR's northern regions. Instead, the vernalized crops failed, contributing to the widespread hunger.

Under the centralized system of farming, workers had little incentive to perform well, and even in years when the harvest promised to be good, much of it was lost to poor practices in the field and along the entire chain of distribution. The only program that kept more people from starving was the government's decision to allow collective farm workers to cultivate their own small plots, which often made the difference between life and death.

The Siege of Leningrad

In June 1941 the Germans invaded the Soviet Union, and by September 8, 1941, they had surrounded Leningrad (formerly Saint Petersburg), Russia's great imperial capital and the second largest city in the land. The subsequent siege lasted for nearly nine hundred days. Roughly one million Leningraders died as a result of the Wehrmacht's intentional policy of starvation.

An immediate target of the German bombing campaign was Leningrad's Badaev warehouses, where stores of flour and sugar were kept. The warehouses were completely destroyed, but after the conflagrations were extinguished, workers managed to salvage a quantity of the 2,500 tons of sugar that had melted onto the ground, turning the thick, black syrup into candy. Seven hundred tons of sugar were lost, as well as all of the flour. It was a severe blow to a population already hungry from the war rations that had been imposed since June, particularly as temperatures dropped and heating fuel became unavailable. Resourceful Leningraders used axes to loosen the frozen soil saturated with sugar. Certain enterprising individuals made a profit on this "sweet earth," selling soil that had been retrieved down to a depth of three feet for one hundred rubles a glass; soil from farther beneath the surface cost only fifty rubles. People heated the soil and strained the melted sugar through muslin, or mixed it with library paste to make a gummy confection. Some simply ate the earth, washing it down with hot water.

As months passed, the proportion of flour used in bakery loaves kept diminishing. In mid-September, fodder oats and malt had been added to the commercial bread recipe. In late October, moldy grain retrieved from a sunken ship in Lake Ladoga was dried out and added to the dough. On November 20, 1941, the government reduced the already meager bread ration. Factory workers were allotted 250 grams a day; all others received a mere 125 grams, about one-quarter of a pound. The loaf's composition was standardized at 73 percent rye flour, 10 percent "edible" cellulose, 10 percent cottonseed-oil cake (*zhmykh*, normally used as animal feed), 2 percent chaff, 2 percent flour sweepings and dust shaken from flour sacks, and 3 percent corn flour. Siege bread was damp, heavy, and greenish-brown, its texture so crumbly that it fell apart in the hands, even as each crumb felt unpleasantly gummy. It tasted terrible. The dense fillers also made this siege loaf 68 percent heavier than a normal loaf of bread, so a 125-gram ration contained only 74.4 grams of digestible matter. Other foods were necessary to supplement the scanty bread ration, but during that first fall and winter of the siege, virtually no other food was available. Nursing mothers were so malnourished that they could no longer produce milk, but the authorities allocated only 3½ ounces of soy milk for infants per day. One mother wrote of nicking her arm to draw blood to give her baby something to suck on. Women braved artillery fire as they searched for food. At night, dressed in dark clothes, they ventured out into the fields and chopped at the frozen earth to dig any potatoes left rotting underground.

Desperate Leningraders collected flour dust from cracks in the kitchen floorboards and licked spattered grease from kitchen walls. They tore books apart for the glue from their bindings and scraped wallpaper paste from the walls (the glue and paste were made from

FIGURE 9. Sergei Blokhin, Blockade bread ration of 125 grams, 1941. During the worst months of the siege of Leningrad, the daily bread ration for ordinary citizens was a mere 125 grams—just over one-quarter pound. The coarse rye bread was no supplement to other rations; it was the only food the government made available, and losing a ration coupon could spell death. Collection of the Multimedia Art Museum, Moscow.

animal protein). They turned joiner's glue into a semblance of aspic by soaking it for twenty-four hours, then boiling it long and hard, releasing a terrible odor of burnt horns and hooves. When the glue cooled, it thickened. A bit of vinegar or mustard made it barely palatable.

The winter of 1942 proved to be one of the century's harshest, aggravating the famine conditions, since cold weather requires people to ingest more calories to survive. But the frigid temperatures also provided a slim lifeline when the waters of Lake Ladoga froze. Engineers, along with ice fishermen who knew the lake's hazardous spots, mapped out a transport route across the thick ice and cleared it with snowplows. The ice road, which the hungry inhabitants called the Road of Life, stretched for twenty-nine kilometers (eighteen miles). Because it lay only twelve to fifteen miles from German-occupied territory, it was under constant threat of artillery fire. Nevertheless, heavy trucks plied the road day and night, bringing flour to the starving city as well as some medical and military supplies. On the return trip the trucks evacuated women, children, wounded soldiers, and some of the great works of art from the Hermitage. The journey was fraught with danger, compounded by high lake-effect winds, and many people died trying to make the crossing. In the first two weeks alone, nearly two hundred trucks sank through the ice. After the ice melted in the spring, the Road of Life operated with ships until winter convoys resumed in December 1942. All told, more than 1.5 million tons of food were transported along the route, and nearly 1.5 million people escaped from the city.

Those who remained suffered terribly. Many died during the first winter from starvation or the cold. When the spring of 1942 finally arrived, the survivors foraged for anything green. Grass disappeared from the parks, as did the tiny new leaves on trees. Women made tasty, vitamin-rich soup from nettles and dandelion leaves and ground the dandelion roots into flour for pancakes to supplement the still-meager rations. These urbanites learned harsh lessons in subsistence, including how to forage for plants they had not known to be edible. Not all behaved nobly. Although nothing good should be said about siege existence, from a societal perspective it offered interesting moments. Lidiya Ginzburg, in her brilliant and unflinching *Blockade Diary,* writes about how food and conversations about it transcended the usual barriers of gender and class. Whereas Soviet intellectuals had generally considered domestic issues beneath them, siege life gave them new preoccupations: "This conversation [about food], which had previously drawn down the scorn of men and businesswomen (especially young ones) and which [the housewife] had been forbidden to inflict upon the thinking man—this conversation had triumphed. It had taken on a universal social meaning and importance, paid for by the terrible experience of the winter."

Soviet "Deficits"

Long after the end of World War II, an economy of scarcity—"deficits" in Soviet parlance—still prevailed in the Soviet Union. When equipment broke down on the massive state-run farms, there were typically no spare parts. Thus seeds didn't get sown on time, and fields were not harvested when the crops were ripe. Sometimes the equipment was operational, but there was no fuel. Graft, inefficiency, and the central planning bureaucracy discouraged both problem-solving and innovation. The Central Committee's solution was "volunteer" labor. Each autumn at potato harvesting time, high school and university students, workers, and engineers were required to interrupt their normal lives and travel as far as Siberia to dig potatoes for hours on end in cold and wet weather. The camaraderie of the adventure sometimes compensated for the difficult labor, as did the opportunity to purloin produce to take home. But even this increased workforce couldn't ensure that potatoes got to market. The distribution network was so poorly organized that an overabundance of any crop from one region of the vast USSR could not be shipped to another region where the harvest had been poor. Moreover, there was little incentive to create value-added products. Food simply went to waste.

To compensate for the country's considerable agricultural shortfalls, Russians had to import grain, and beginning in 1963, most of it came, humiliatingly, from the United States. Calamitous harvests in 1972 and 1975—the result of both weather and the systemic inefficiencies of centralized planning—necessitated the import of record amounts of grain. In 1976 the Soviets and Americans negotiated a grain deal that lasted over a decade, in which Moscow agreed to buy a minimum of six million tons of American wheat and corn each year. Much of the imported wheat was earmarked for human consumption (Soviet yields had been not only low but also of poor quality), although some also went for cattle feed as livestock production in the Soviet Union increased. In the marketing year 1979–80, the Soviet Union imported roughly thirty million tons of grain from the US.

This number suggests dire circumstances. But in fact Soviet citizens were not starving: their average calorie intake was sufficient, even if their diet was lacking in protein and other nutrients. The problem was more an issue of societal expectations. In the mid-1930s Stalin had responded to discontent by jump-starting a manufacturing plan to make consumer luxury products like chocolate and inexpensive champagne accessible to all. In 1936 Anastas Mikoyan, the minister for the food industry, spent two months in the US studying mass production. He brought back equipment for making ice cream, cornflakes, and hamburgers on an industrial scale.

World War II derailed the burgeoning hamburger industry, but when Nikita Khrushchev came to power in 1953, he worked hard to increase meat production. Like Mikoyan, Khrushchev visited the United States and returned with plans for an aggressive campaign to plant corn as cattle fodder throughout the Soviet Union. In 1964 he even commissioned the first commercial to appear on Russian television: an astonishing and surreal two-minute operetta promoting the consumption of corn, which contributed to his eventual nickname, "Nikita Corn Man" (Nikita Kukuruznik). The campaign failed, as did his misguided campaign to plant wheat in the arid "virgin lands" of Kazakhstan and the Altai region. One relative success was his 1961 initiative to develop the fishing industry by seeding Kamchatka crabs from the north Pacific in the Barents Sea. Suddenly, cans of Chatka crab were plentiful in the stores, though many of the enormous crabs themselves, whose leg span reaches up to six feet, ultimately defected, swimming to freedom in Norwegian waters, where they devastated indigenous species and continue to threaten the vital cod industry there.

Overall the Soviet diet remained dreary and monotonous. Eating major meals out was rarely an option, apart from quick bites at casual places like tearooms, where savory pies could be had with a cup of tea for under a ruble. With food-service recipes standardized by the state, there was little motivation for inventiveness or maintaining quality. Even the names of the cafeterias were dispiriting, often consisting of a number only, such as Cafeteria No. 11. People craved more variety and better food, but also more panache. Increasing prosperity meant that people had the means to buy better food, but for ordinary Soviet citizens there was little available. A triad of food-related issues defined the late Soviet era: enduring scarcity; a desire for luxury foods and the prestige associated with them; and the creativity with which people tackled home cooking and provisioning. Home cooks displayed great ingenuity in making decorative and tasty composed salads from otherwise mundane canned fish, and *kotlety* from minced vegetables like mushrooms and carrots instead of meat. Ordinary Russians prepared astonishingly beautiful meals on two-burner stoves in kitchens the size of closets.

Of necessity, Soviet citizens lived and breathed sustainability. Everything was recycled; even bits of string were saved. There was no aluminum foil, no plastic wrap, no extraneous packaging. Coveted plastic bags were reused until they shredded. Milk was often bought at distribution points where it was poured into bottles that were returned for refilling. Old nylon stockings were repurposed for keeping onions; they allowed for good airflow and could be hung to free up the limited storage space in urban apartments. Stockings were also an excellent substitute for cheesecloth when making farmer's cheese or straining jelly. Conversely, sugar did double duty as hairspray when mixed with water. And because fine store-bought candies were expensive—their very names, like Bird's Milk and Daydream, signaling how difficult they were to procure—sugar was melted at home to a very dark caramel stage to make burnt-sugar hard candies—a use oddly reminiscent of the blockade, without the anguish. Favorite pastries were the "potatoes" and "sausages" made from crushed cookie crumbs, condensed milk, cocoa, butter, and sometimes ground walnuts.

The burdens of domestic life fell almost entirely on women, even though they made up half of the workforce. In families in which several generations lived together, the grandmother would step into the role of cook and childcare provider. In the postwar years, many women in their twenties and thirties did not want to spend as much time in the kitchen as their mothers and grandmothers had. Tired after a long day of work and a struggle on multiple modes of crowded public transportation, they would often throw things together for a quick supper, since the working adults and schoolchildren in the household had likely eaten a solid mid-day meal at the workplace or school cafeteria. The recipes in cook-books and women's magazines tended to be quick and economical rather than inspirational. Yet for special occasions these same reluctant cooks would pull out the stops, scour the city for delica-cies, and indulge in culinary whimsy, like shaping mundane liver pâté into little hedgehogs replete with butter quills. Even under dif-ficult circumstances, Russians know how to celebrate.

Getting Food, Soviet Style

State-run stores were shabby, depressing outlets for wizened veg-etables and staples like flour, sunflower oil, and dried noodles. Most of these shops sold a specific category of food and, like the cafeterias, were identified only by the generic name of what was supposed to be available inside: Milk, Dairy Products, Fish, Vegetables and Fruits, Groceries, Bread, and so on. Occasional attempts were made at more evocative names, like Ocean and Gifts of the Sea instead of just Fish. But such names remained aspi-rational, as the offerings inside were no more abundant or fresh. Soviet citizens spent hours every day on their quests for food. The vocabulary of Soviet life expressed this reality: many goods could not simply be bought (*kupit'*); they had to be obtained (*dostat'*), a word that signified the many hardships involved in a transaction, whether traveling a long distance, negotiating a complex barter, or trading on the black market.

There existed a few consumer cooperatives (*potrebkooperatsii*), where people could sell their homegrown products. Prices were considerably higher than in the regular state-run stores, but shelves were not empty; even meat was available. The cooperatives were intended as an outlet to thwart black-market profiteering. This strategy didn't fully succeed, since so-called "speculators" could get higher prices on the black market, where they could also exchange their food for some other deficit item. Nevertheless, the co-ops provided an important source of food in rural areas, where state stores were literally few and far between. That dearth prompted country dwellers to head to Moscow, which had priority in food distribution as in everything else in the Soviet Union. Trains arrived daily in the capital filled with villagers who bought up as much as they could lug home in huge carryalls and burlap sacks. Muscovites resented these "sausage trains" for contributing to their own food shortages. "What is long and green and smells like sausage?" went a popular riddle from the Soviet years. The answer: "A train from Moscow."

Here is how a typical shopping foray in the city proceeded, even when there was no queue to get inside the shop. The first step was to shoulder your way to the counter, where goods were displayed in a vitrine or on shelves behind the counter—just to find out what was available. Next it was necessary to get the saleswoman's attention and ask for the desired product. She calculated the price on a wooden abacus and wrote up a sales slip, which you took to a cashier in another part of the store. The cashier rang up the sale and returned a receipt, which had to be brought back to the original salesperson in exchange for the purchase. So a single purchase entailed three steps, and often three queues. If the store was large enough to have several different food sections, this three-stage process had to be repeated for each purchase. So, for instance, separate chits would be required to buy candy, buckwheat groats, and farmer's cheese in their respective sections. This process took considerable time. Because people couldn't simply leave work to spend hours food shopping, they often delegated one person from the office or institute as the shopper of the day. She would use her lunchtime to buy food for her colleagues as well as for her family. In her 1969 novella, *A Week Like Any Other*, Natalia Baranskaya describes the strain of this task: not only lugging heavy shopping bags but also enduring the derision of those who stood in line awaiting their turn, who would rain down insults on the shopper for buying so many groceries. If people couldn't work out a shared system of shopping, they fit it in whenever they could, on their way home from work or on Saturdays, spending much of their "leisure" time running from one store to another searching for food.

The exception to this system was the bakeries, where you could choose from a variety of breads on display and pay for your purchase right at the service counter. In addition, by the mid-1960s a few self-service grocery stores (*universamy*) had opened, where consumers themselves could pick products from the shelves, place them in a shopping basket, and bring them to a central point for checkout. Harried women frequented a type of store known as the *kulinariia,* which sold prepared foods (usually delicious) to take home and heat for dinner. And there were street kiosks strategically placed in front of the stores, or street vendors' stands on sidewalks or in the passageways under busy thoroughfares, where quick purchases could be made on the way home.

Although no stores were privately owned, a calibrated hierarchy prevailed. At the top, accessible only to the Soviet elite, were a handful of stores where deficit items could be reliably found; these were the Beriozka stores that accepted only foreign currency or special certificates. Well-off consumers lacking legal access to either form of currency could shop in the famous Eliseev food halls in Leningrad and Moscow, first established in the nineteenth century. (In Soviet times, despite its official name of Gastronom No. 1, Muscovites continued to refer to the store as Eliseev's.) Prices were high. But even if most people couldn't afford such luxury items as fine caviar, imported sausage, chocolates, liqueurs, and coffee, they could still admire the stunning Art Nouveau interior, which had survived revolution and war.

Palatial food stores with ornamentation and even fountains had also been constructed in the new provincial towns built from scratch in the 1930s, to celebrate the "better, more joyous life" Stalin had decreed. In Moscow, a second fancy food hall, known, like Eliseev's, as Gastronom No. 1, opened in 1953 in the famous department store, GUM, under the direction of Anastas Mikoyan. The store's prices put its wares similarly out of reach for most consumers, but once inside the doors, everyone could head for the affordable ice cream produced in GUM's own facility. Served in a waffle cone, this irresistible ice cream was considered the best in the USSR. Residents of the new, outlying urban districts created in the 1960s to provide mass housing were less fortunate than those living near the center. The rapid construction projects for vast apartment blocks often failed to incorporate food stores, leaving the inhabitants without any nearby source of groceries.

Farmer's markets were another relatively expensive option. Here shoppers could find a cornucopia of produce for sale by vendors from Georgia and Azerbaijan, who regularly boarded inexpensive flights to Moscow, crowding the aisles with their enormous sacks of citrus and semitropical fruits like feijoa. Central Asian vendors offered numerous varieties of raisins and sultanas, dried apricots, dates, and nuts, while Uzbek Koreans sold prepared foods like spicy marinated carrot salad, which had become a beloved feature of the Russian table. Displays of pickled cucumbers, beets, cabbage, and garlic extended the length of the market, as did the dairy products—fine- and coarse-textured farmer's cheese (*tvorog*), sour cream thick and thin, yogurt-like *prostokvasha* and *riazhenka*. Mounds of colorful spices and fresh herbs gave off heady aromas, while flies buzzed around displays of freshly butchered meat.

There also existed informal networks of exchange, a vast and complicated system based on personal acquaintances, favors traded, and perks of the workplace, all of which reflected the *blat,* or connections, that ultimately determined how well most people ate. Virtually everyone engaged in strategic bartering, a Soviet version of "you scratch my back and I'll scratch yours," as each person offered whatever goods they had access to in exchange for the otherwise unobtainable. Access to food also depended on status. Prestigious workplaces and organizations offered their members special "rations" (*payok*) as a perk, through a system of "closed distribution" that guaranteed access to scarce or high-quality foods through vouchers or a salary deduction. These perks might include black caviar, citrus fruits, and bananas, all in short supply; often there were coveted foreign packaged goods, too. The best institutions had their own dining rooms, which sometimes allowed their members to bring food home. People associated with a prestigious organization, or who lived in an elite apartment block, could also avoid queues by placing orders for home delivery at distribution points that were unknown to the general public.

Such food distribution systems were, of course, inequitable, but they were also social. Your office, factory, or neighborhood was your tribe. Buying food was a national obsession and, for most people, a slog. Word of mouth was all-important, and Soviet shoppers developed a kind of sixth sense. Even if, say, no sausage was visible in a store, an extra-large crowd milling about likely meant that sausage was about to appear, so it was worth joining the throng. Shipments of deficit items were carried out in secrecy, but someone inevitably knew someone involved in the transport, or who worked at the store and would share insider information. This information was passed on selectively to others, and in this way a lively network of rumors developed, which not infrequently proved to be fact. People rarely left home without a string bag (aptly named an *avos'ka,* "just in case"), lest they miss an opportunity to buy deficit items that could appear unpredictably and disappear just as quickly. If they had somehow forgotten a bag, they scrambled to get old newspapers from kiosks to wrap up their unexpected purchases. Savvy shoppers knew not to visit a shop during its regular hours but to get in line during the hour-long closure for lunch, because deficit items were most likely to appear just after the shop reopened. When a product did suddenly materialize, lines formed in an instant. Some queues—so-called "living" ones—could stretch for several kilometers. Hours could pass before you actually reached the store, hours filled with anxiety that the product would run out before you got in the door.

Imported foods were especially prized, sometimes more for their shiny packaging than for their quality. In her short story "Puffed Rice and Meatballs," the émigré writer Lara Vapnyar describes this feature of Soviet life:

> [Vera's] forehead was covered with sweat and her eyes bulged with excitement; she clearly was oblivious to everything in the world. . . .
>
> 'Puffed . . . puffed . . . puffed rice,' she panted. 'They are selling puffed rice in the Littlestore.' She clutched my sleeve and tried to

catch a breath. 'American puffed rice in crunchy bags? A friend of my mother's hairdresser told us. We have to run because the line is getting bigger every second.' . . .

We were two hundred fifty-sixth and two hundred fifty-seventh in the line. The reason we knew was that they scribbled the numbers in blue ink right on our palms. I had to keep my marked hand apart, so the number wouldn't rub off accidentally, as happened to a woman who stood ahead of us. She kept showing her sweaty palm to everybody and asking if they could still read her number, when there wasn't anything but a faded blue stain. I was sure they would turn her away from the counter.

The legendary queues of the late Soviet period were a grueling waste of people's time. And yet, at its best, the queue offered an opportunity to share knowledge and represented a kind of societal communion. Describing the siege of Leningrad, Lidiya Ginzburg wrote about how the queue broke down differences between intellectuals—who had never bothered to think seriously about food— and peasants, who were able to impart folk wisdom about extracting nutrients from unlikely sources, based on their historical experience of hunger. Standing in line enabled a truer collective than the stratified, secretive Soviet state.

Still, as often as not the queue provoked anxiety and bad behavior, adding to the stress of daily life. Access to food became even more difficult in the mid-1980s, during perestroika, when the state began issuing ration coupons for products like butter and sausage, often euphemistically offering an "invitation to receive" a specific amount of a certain product. By the end of the 1980s, shortly before the Soviet Union collapsed, the government was rationing even basic necessities like buckwheat groats, salt, vegetable oil, and tea.

Many people tried to game the system by buying things they didn't need and reselling them at a profit, or simply by selling the ration coupons for profit. The great paradox of Soviet life was that even though the stores were visibly empty, everything was available, one way or another.

Dacha Gardens

The only sure way to guarantee the availability of staples like potatoes was to grow them yourself. Most of the population, including a great many city dwellers, cultivated their own garden plots, which allowed them to endure periods of food shortages. These private plots, worked in off-hours and on weekends, created a significant second economy—one that the government came increasingly to rely on, since the collective and state farms never managed to meet the nation's demand for fresh produce. Potatoes topped the list of home-grown foods. While it had taken several imperial edicts and not a few riots before the tuber was finally established, during the Soviet years the potato became the essential garden crop, affording a sense of security: as long as there was a potato harvest, a family would not starve. Most families also grew onions, radishes, scallions, and garlic; cucumbers and beets; tomatoes; and abundant herbs, especially dill. Rural inhabitants were allowed to keep a pig, a cow for milk, and some chickens for eggs. Going to the dacha also enabled people to forage in the countryside for the mushrooms and berries that remain crucial components of the Russian diet.

The dacha—a country residence that can range from a manor to a shack—has a long history in Russian life. The practice of handing out land as a mark of favor from the tsar dates back to the sixteenth century. Peter the Great expanded and institutionalized

FIGURE 10. Mikhail Grachev, *Making Jam at the Dacha,*
1950s. The Russian love for life at the dacha is captured in
this image of a woman taking advantage of summer's boun-
teous berries to make jam outdoors. Collection of the Multimedia Art Museum, Moscow.

this practice as he set about creating suburban residences for
court favorites in his new city of Saint Petersburg. These early
dachas, intended for aristocratic leisure away from the noise and
pollution of the city, were often quite grand. By the nineteenth
century the dacha was firmly established in Russian upper-
and middle-class life. In Soviet times, retreating to a dacha on

weekends was considered a healthful activity. These dachas were often little more than uninsulated cottages, with no plumbing or electricity, which entailed constant improvement. Dacha gardens had always been part of the pleasure of escaping to the countryside, but as the twentieth century progressed, they became crucial to survival.

A small number of garden plots existed within city limits, but most lay well beyond. Beginning at the spring planting season, urban dwellers took weekend trains to the countryside to work the land. In late summer they hauled sacks of produce back to the city to make gallons of pickles and preserves, which were then stored in all the odd corners of their apartments, under sofa beds and on window ledges. The phrase "at the dacha" evokes an immediate connection to the rhythms of nature and to being Russian, while also suggesting a source of security in a country where social upheaval and hunger remain within memory. Russians are devoted to their dachas not only because they offer respite from urban life, but because they enable self-reliance. Yet maintaining a garden was hardly romantic. Getting to some rural plots required hours of travel first by train and then by bus, with the final distance covered on foot. Because the countryside had few amenities, food for the entire weekend had to be packed and transported. Nevertheless, in the face of the country's agricultural failures, harvesting your own produce was well worth the effort.

Most garden plots allotted to urban families were six *sotka*s (about one-seventh of an acre) in size. Those who lived in the countryside, or who worked on collective or state farms, had larger plots. Factories were also given land that was turned into gardening cooperatives for their workers. Throughout the Soviet period, all land was owned by the government, but any buildings on it—storage sheds or shacks that people gradually turned into livable dwellings—belonged to whoever had built them, and they could be sold or passed on to the next generation. Private plots accounted for an astonishing amount of produce, between one-quarter and one-third of the Soviet Union's agricultural output throughout the 1970s and 1980s. And although the state never published official data, it is believed that by the last years of Soviet rule, up to 90 percent of the country's fresh vegetables, as well as significant amounts of meat and dairy products, came either from dacha gardens or from the small plots allotted to collective-farm and factory workers. In the chaos that followed the collapse of the Soviet Union and its centralized system of agriculture, dacha gardens and the sharing economy saved the populace from famine. Most dacha produce was consumed by the family or shared with others; only secondarily was it sold on the local markets for cash, although in the early post-Soviet years, with a newly destitute rural population, old women sitting at the side of a road selling a few berries or herbs or jars of jam were a heartbreaking and all-too-frequent sight.

The Soviet Kitchen

In urban areas, many families lived in communal apartments—formerly large apartments that had been divided up among numerous families, each of whom had a single room that served as living room, dining room, and bedroom. The hallway, toilet, and kitchen were all shared spaces. To avoid conflict, families staggered cooking times at the kitchen's multiple stoves. For obvious reasons, they kept small refrigerators in their own rooms (those lucky enough to have bought the large models released in the 1950s had to keep

FIGURE 11. Pavel Kassin, *Municipal Apartment from a Soviet Childhood,* Moscow, 1983. Communal kitchens could have several stoves and sinks, depending on how many families lived in the apartment, and each family was sometimes assigned specific burners and basins. Squabbles often arose when someone trespassed onto another person's space. Because the kitchen also served as a laundry room, it was impossible to maintain a fully private life. Photograph courtesy of Pavel Kassin.

them literally under lock and key in the communal kitchen). Often filthy and overrun with cockroaches, the communal kitchen was typically a dehumanizing space that upended any notion of kitchen as the physical and emotional heart of a home.

For those fortunate enough to have their own apartment, and thus their own space, the kitchen took on larger meaning. The intelligentsia frequently entertained at a small, oilcloth-covered table that did double duty as a work surface, gathering for conversation after having carefully removed the telephone to another room and covered it with a pillow for fear of being bugged, or turning on the water in the sink to muffle any words. These conversations constituted a kind of kitchen dissidence, the late-twentieth-century equivalent of literary and intellectual salons, where people spoke more freely after a glass or two of vodka and read forbidden works of samizdat aloud from poor carbon copies or played contraband musical recordings. The kitchen was the one place where people could freely meet without observation, and in this way the Soviet kitchen kept Russian culture alive. The kitchen table defied the constraints of a life defined by scarcity, as abundant vodka and food invariably appeared on the table. Friends crowded in, sitting on stools and laps, often with a dozen adults and children crammed into only five or six square meters. The impromptu meals of hearty black bread, tins of canned fish, and home-salted mushrooms pulled from the stash under the bed, accompanied as they were by a lively exchange of ideas, represented an undeniable triumph over adversity, a genuine, loving communality.

3   *Hospitality and Excess*

The kulebiaka should be appetizing, shameless in its nakedness, a temptation to sin. You wink at it, slice an oh-so-big piece and run your fingers over it from an excess of emotion. You start eating, and butter flows like tears, the filling is rich, luscious, with eggs, giblets, onions.

ANTON CHEKHOV, "The Siren"

Hospitality is no abstraction in Russian culture. It takes material form as a large, round loaf of bread, milled from the finest flour, with an indentation for a small dish of salt. The presentation of this *khleb da sol',* bread and salt, is a gesture of welcome from which the word *khlebosol'stvo,* "hospitality," derives. In proffering bread and salt, Russians offer the most basic sustenance along with a precious foodstuff (salt was once very expensive), in a deeply traditional, near-sacred act.

The sharing of bread and salt was considered especially important at liminal moments: at weddings, when the social status of bride and groom shifted; at housewarmings, when new thresholds were crossed; and when new tsars were crowned. At Tsar Alexander III's coronation in 1883, delegates from far and wide presented him with bread and salt displayed on exquisitely crafted platters of precious metals, which were subsequently transferred to the Kremlin Armory for safekeeping. Bread and salt reflect both a Christian sacrament—bread symbolizes the body of Christ—and superstitious belief. Russians invoked bread and salt as protection against evil spirits, to the point of uttering the words "*khleb da sol*'" at the end of a meal to ensure that no harm would come to those assembled. Monasteries used to bless a large loaf of rye bread to send as a benediction to the tsar's table. The tsar, in turn, distributed bread to all those attending his feasts, in strict hierarchical order. Once having partaken of the tsar's bread—and, by extension, of the Lord's blessing—anyone who acted against him was damned.

Hospitality is so central to Russian life that the Russian language has not one but two words for it, the second being *gostepriimstvo*, or the receiving of guests. Guests are always afforded a place of honor at the table. In peasant cottages, that meant seating guests in the "beautiful corner," under the icons and diagonally across from the stove. Even the poorest households offered sustenance not just to friends but also to strangers. For the devout peasant, hospitality was a simple and heartfelt, even devotional, act.

Two essential components of Russian hospitality reveal its underpinnings for the peasantry and aristocracy: *dobrodushie* (cordiality), which has as its root the word "soul," and *userdie* (zeal), etymologically formed from the word "heart" plus an amplifying prefix. For the peasants, hospitality extended naturally from devotion to God. Treating guests well was an end in itself. But for those with greater means, the zeal for overindulging often caused the vaunting of luxury foods and extravagant settings to supplant the act of hospitality.

For the tsar and much of the aristocracy, the more theatrical and public their displays of generosity, the greater the pleasure they derived from them. In medieval times, the tsar showed his favor to noblemen and foreign emissaries alike by sending a *podacha*, a lavish gift of food and drink from his table, to their residence, even if they had dined with him. This singular form of Russian generosity captured the attention of the French mercenary Jacques Margaret, who lived in Muscovy from 1600 to 1606. He was struck not just by the graciousness of the gesture, but also by its excess. Margaret describes processions that involved three or four hundred men parading through Moscow's streets bearing food and drink. They processed after a "chief gentleman" on horseback, dressed "in cloth of gold, his mantle and hat decorated with pearls." Six men carried bread; drinks were so abundant that a dozen men were needed to carry large silver vessels of foreign wines, while forty more men carried various meads. Meats and pies (which could easily number one hundred dishes) were held aloft on platters of silver, or sometimes of gold, if the guest was especially honored. Such street theater performances could occur several times a day and were not always welcomed by the recipients, who found them burdensome; according to the rules of Russian hospitality, it was incumbent upon them to accept the tsar's gift. As for the spectators, they were present for more than the pageantry alone: in an expression of royal largesse, the procession dispensed free mead and beer. Thus the *podacha*s offered a double release valve for the masses' privations, giving them both spectacle and libations and thereby making them less likely to rebel.

In their memoirs and travelogues, foreign envoys to Muscovy often complained about having to endure official feasts at the tsar's table, where they were unaccustomed to the formal progression of the meal. The Russian practice of serving courses sequentially (which came to be known as *service à la russe,* in the Russian style) contrasted greatly with the classical French-style banquet, an exquisite set piece intended to delight the eye. French banquet tables displayed the artistry of geometrically arranged dishes whose pattern was never disturbed, despite the changing of courses. The visual effect was dazzling, but a preset display, left at room temperature for hours, ran the risk of causing food poisoning. By contrast, the Russian style of service both kept the food hot and added a measure of surprise. But because multicourse feasts could drag on for hours, visitors never knew how much food to expect, and some foreign envoys found the uncertainty unnerving. The feast that Tsar Alexei Mikhailovich held on February 19, 1664, in honor of the Earl of Carlisle, who was in Muscovy as an envoy of King Charles II, lasted from two in the afternoon till eleven at night. Carlisle's secretary left a vivid description:

> At last the *Stolnicks* entred, with their great bonnets upon their heads, and brought the first meat to the *Tzars* Table, presently afterwards they served the *Boyars,* and then my Lord Ambassador and his Train. Our first dish was Caviare, which we eat as a Sallad, after which we had a sort of Pottage that was very sweet, as also several sorts of fish baked, fried, and boyled; but no flesh, because it was Lent. Yet that hindered not but that we had near five hundred dishes, which were very handsomely dressed, had not the dishes been so very black, that they looked more like Lead than Silver. Of all these dishes they made as it were but one course, new coming in continually; but as we had no napkins allowed us, so wanted we but little of having no plates also . . . Besides these we

were well provided with very good *Spanish* Wine, white and red Mead; Quaz [kvass], and strong Waters, which they had tempered with sweet and odoriferous ingredients. . . . By this time the *desart* came in, and the *Tzar* invited the Ambassador to take his place at the Table again. The first things they brought in, were little artificial trees with store of branches candyed and guilt at the ends, on purpose for a shew; the rest were nothing but a kind of fritters, wafers, and such like trifles in paste, made up after their fashion.

Exorbitant Illusion

With attention focused on table service, rather than on any extrinsic entertainment such as musical interludes, the elite Russian meal was in itself a performance. Russia certainly had its share of dwarves and jesters to entertain guests (their antics were particularly enjoyed by Peter the Great, who had naked dwarves instead of blackbirds "baked" into pies), but the Russian aristocracy did not develop the art of mealtime pageantry as diversion, as was the custom in Western Europe. And because the needs of the gentry were largely taken care of by the many serfs they owned, the gentry had plenty of time to dream up grand, inventive dinners that helped dispel boredom. Mikhail Pyliaev, in his study *The Old Way of Life* (*Staroe zhit'yo,* 1892), documented the dinner parties of some of Moscow's most hospitable—and unconventional—hosts, who often relied on illusion for maximum effect. At one memorable meal, Count Alexander Sergeevich Stroganov decorated his dining room to recall ancient Rome, with swansdown-stuffed pillows and mattresses arranged around a triclinium where his guests—all male—could recline during the meal, like the dissolute ancients. Each guest was served by a graceful boy who carried in one exquisite dish after another, Russian style. Appetizers consisted of caviar, radishes, plums, and imported pomegranates; most extravagant of all were the herring cheeks, for which more than one thousand herrings were needed to yield a single serving. The second course included salmon lips, boiled bears' paws, and roast lynx. Cuckoos roasted in honey and butter, wildfowl stuffed with nuts and fresh figs, cod milt, turbot liver, oysters, salted peaches, and pickled hothouse pineapples rounded out the meal. Whenever his guests felt full, Stroganov, like Roman hosts before him, encouraged them to tickle their throats with a feather to vomit and make room for more. After the meal, the diners drank in the Russian style, eating salty pressed caviar as they steamed in the *banya*, which had the benefit of piquing their thirst.

Pyliaev further recounts the mischievous hospitality of the well-known eccentric Prokofy Demidov, whose magnificent gardens featured over two thousand rare plants. Demidov allowed his dinner guests to wander freely among them, but for one dinner party, after his female guests had plucked too many fruits and flowers, he replaced the garden statuary with naked peasant men. The filching stopped. On the eve of another gathering, he had painters whitewash every room, except for the dining room, and place scaffolding in front of every door. When the guests arrived in their finest attire, Demidov apologized for the scaffolding that forced his guests to contort their way around crude obstacles until they finally reached the dining room, where the doors opened to a splendid meal. A predilection for comedy is evident in the evenings orchestrated by noblemen eccentric and otherwise, who sought to counter the frequent isolation imposed by distance and weather by amusing their guests in unexpected ways. At the same time they took pleasure in competing with one another to demonstrate outrageousness and profligacy. According to Pyliaev, the renowned gastronome Nikita Vsevolozhsky would invite 120 guests to his holiday meals, at which he served fresh hothouse strawberries in December and fish that had been flash-frozen and transported to Saint Petersburg from the distant Urals—including one fish so large that it took four dozen kitchen serfs to parade it around the table on their shoulders before carrying it back to the kitchen for portioning.

Such spendthrift behavior was not uncommon among the nobility, and numerous broadsides or *lubki*, a form of folk art popular in Russia from the seventeenth to nineteenth centuries, addressed this extravagance. Originally printed from incised wood and then colored by hand with tempera paints, woodblock *lubki* increasingly gave way to colored engravings as printing technology progressed, and by the late nineteenth century they were mass-produced by chromolithography. *Lubki* treated many subjects, from edifying religious themes and folk mythology to political and social concerns. In almost all cases the imagery was accompanied by text, often in the form of verse.

One widely disseminated *lubok*, "The Feast of the Pious and the Profane," dates from the late seventeenth or early eighteenth century. Its cutaway architectural view depicts two groups of people feasting in Muscovite-style chambers. Pagan and Christian iconography mingle as an anthropomorphic sun looks out from the upper left-hand corner, while the figure of Christ appears in a cartouche on the right. In the top center of the illustration, pious diners feast at a table presided over by a guardian angel, enjoying their meal close to heaven, near the figure of Christ. The angel holds a long spear whose point is visible under the table, where a demon lies slain. The pious diners remain focused on their meal, their hands reaching for simple bread and perhaps fish on one of the few plates that appear on the spare table. Significantly, there are no utensils, reflecting the idea that our hands are God-given tools for eating that keep us connected to our source of sustenance. Neither is there any sign of drink at the table. This *lubok* is based on the homilies of Saint John Chrysostom, who equated luxurious food with prostitution and indolence; it also echoes the rules for moral living laid out in Russia's sixteenth-century household manual, the *Domostroi*, reminding people to conduct themselves right-eously at table.

Just below the pious diners, at a more lavishly set table, an impi-ous company consorts with demons. The *lubok*'s text describes this group as ungrateful, idle blasphemers and foul-mouthed liars. Their table is set with various utensils, including forks, which the early church associated with the devil because of their tines, seen as an abstraction of the devil's horns. The revelers are surrounded by winged demons, one of which is actually defecating into a bowl on the table. The demons carry staffs that look like hooks, a sym-bolic representation of their ability to lure people into temptation. Temptation exists here in the form of the woman seated at the table, as well as in the minstrels in the lower right-hand corner, whose playing on lute and bagpipes serves as a distraction from what should be a sacred meal. A carafe on the table indicates the consumption of spirits. The guardian angel is seen fleeing from this feast, distraught at such goings-on.

However, for aristocratic Russians, the kind of parsimonious approach to the table urged by this *lubok* held little or no appeal. Starting in the late eighteenth century, in both Moscow and Saint Petersburg, a fashion for "open tables" took hold among high soci-ety, at which anyone of the proper class was welcome to appear for

FIGURE 12. *Lubok* of *The Feast of the Pious and the Profane,* late seventeenth or early eighteenth century. Wikimedia Commons.

dinner unannounced, whether they were known to the host or not. With battalions of serfs at the ready, wealthy Russians could easily provide abundant spreads: the only prerequisites were time and money, both of which they possessed in excess. Occasionally traditionalist voices were raised in protest. In his 1787 treatise *On the Corruption of Morals in Russia,* Prince Mikhail Shcherbatov, an early proponent of Russian conservatism, decried the focus on conviviality and rued the loss of the meal's sacred character. He saw open tables as evidence of Russia's moral degeneration, made all the more palpable by the introduction of foreign ingredients:

> The meals were not of the traditional kind, that is, when only household products were used; now they tried to improve the flavor of the meat and fish with foreign seasonings. And of course, in a nation in which hospitality has always been a characteristic virtue, it was not hard for the custom of these open tables to become a habit; uniting as it did the special pleasure of society and the improved flavor of the food as compared with the traditional kind, it established itself as a pleasure in its own right. (trans. A. Lentin)

What troubled Shcherbatov most was the idea of the table as "a pleasure in its own right," with no thought given to the moral obligations of the meal.

The Hospitable Host

The moral duties of hosting were considerable. In Russian, the words "guest" (*gost'*) and "lord" (*gospodin*) share the same root; in welcoming guests and treating them well, the host by extension honors God. Folk belief held that since the Lord Jesus was known to wander the earth, any wayfarer could be the Lord in disguise, and those who treated strangers well would be rewarded. The conviction that "a guest on the threshold brings happiness to the home" extended from wayfaring strangers to invited guests. By welcoming outsiders, Russians rendered the "other" familiar, their own. The guest, in turn, was obligated to accept the host's food and drink. To decline was not just to offend the host but to risk bringing down calamity, perhaps onto the guest himself. Thus moral duties were fulfilled, at least in part, out of a fear of repercussions that reflected both superstitious belief and piety.

In prescribing how to lead a moral life, the *Domostroi* forcefully states the rules of hospitality, couching them in religious terms. One chapter, titled "How You and Your Servants Should Express Gratitude to God While Entertaining Guests," explains that "if those present eat gratefully, in silence or while engaged in devout conversation, the angels will stand by invisibly and write down the diners' good deeds. Their food and drink will be sweet. But if those present utter blasphemy as they begin to eat, the food will turn to dung in their mouths" (trans. Carolyn Johnston Pouncy).

Other chapters advise "How a Man Must Keep Liquor Stored for Himself and His Guests; How to Present This Liquor to Company" and "[How] a Wife Must Consult Her Husband and Ask His Advice Every Day; How a Woman Should Act While Visiting and What She Should Talk about with Guests." Under this latter heading we find (not surprisingly) the following instruction: "If your wife is a guest or has guests herself, she should not get drunk." The book's insistence on propriety and its judgmental tone stand in sharp contrast to the revelry Russians so often engaged in and the extent to which hospitality was expressed in affluent homes.

Indeed, Russian hospitality often shocked foreign visitors to Muscovy, especially the seventeenth-century kissing ritual they encountered in elite homes. Women in these households were kept away from the public eye, in a separate wing of the house called the *terem,* but when an honored guest was in the house, they were commanded to appear. The kissing ritual usually, though not always, took place over the course of a meal. The host's wife (and often his married daughters and servants) was brought out and presented to the guest as a sign of the host's most profound hospitality. The woman then proffered a goblet of vodka, mead, or beer to the guest and allowed him to kiss her on the lips. Adam Olearius, the diplomat from Holstein, experienced this ritual when he visited the Moscow home of Count Lev Alexandrovich Shliakhovsky in 1643:

> After a sumptuous dinner [the Count] called me away from the table and the other guests. He ushered me into another room and said that the greatest honor and favor anyone can be given in Russia is for the mistress of the house to come out and render homage to the guest as to the master. . . . Then his wife came forth. She had a very lovely, but berouged face, and was dressed in her wedding costume. She was accompanied by a maid who carried a bottle of vodka and a cup. Upon her entry she bowed her head first to her husband and then to me. Then she ordered a cup of vodka poured out, took a sip, and handed it to me to drink, repeating this procedure three times. Then the count invited me to kiss her. Since I was unaccustomed to such honors, I kissed only her hand, but he insisted that I kiss her mouth. Accordingly, out of respect to a higher ranking personage, I was obliged to adapt myself to

their custom and accept this honor. (*The Travels of Olearius in Seventeenth-Century Russia*, trans. Samuel H. Baron)

This practice disappeared with Peter the Great's reforms and the subsequent liberation of women from the *terem*. Notably, the cookbooks that appeared beginning in the late eighteenth century omit any specific instructions regarding the reception of guests, even as they comment on table settings, stocking the larder, and training the servants. What they do convey, though, is the firm belief that no expense should be spared for guests, even if it means economizing on family meals, as Elena Molokhovets suggests in her magisterial cookbook, *A Gift to Young Housewives* (1861).

With ten children to feed, Molokhovets had to consider household economy and efficiency, and thanks to her extensive commentary on domestic life and marital harmony, her book proved enormously popular, going through twenty-nine editions before the revolution. The book was then banned for being too bourgeois, but it lived on in legend. A well-stocked larder became the subject of a popular Soviet-era joke, which ascribed to Molokhovets the line "If unexpected guests should arrive, descend to the larder and fetch a cold leg of veal." (Other versions substituted hazel hen, ham, or a leg of lamb for the veal.) People would recite this line, then burst out laughing at the fantastic idea of having that kind of food on hand, not to mention a private cellar for storing it. The reappearance of *A Gift to Young Housewives* after nearly seventy years was a bellwether for the dramatic changes shaking late Soviet life. Under perestroika, in the late 1980s, various recipes of hers had begun to circulate, and a complete reprint of the 1901 edition of her book appeared in 1991, just months before the collapse of the Soviet Union.

The Aesthetics of the Table

After visiting Saint Petersburg in the late 1860s, the French writer Théophile Gautier described in *Voyage en Russie* how he was received by his hosts: "At table, a servant dressed in black, with white cravat and white gloves, as correct in his dress as an English diplomat, stands behind you, imperturbably serious, ready to satisfy your slightest wishes." Having one's own private servant allowed for a dining aesthetic that differed from the European convention. Tables set *à la russe* sparkled with crystal, silver, and porcelain but were nearly devoid of food. Their visual drama lay in highly architectural floral displays or pyramids of costly fruits like oranges, pineapples, and grapes. A typical centerpiece might include a *plateau* or *grand plat de ménage,* a tray of silver or porcelain on which candles were often placed to accentuate the luster. The table itself was laid with a white tablecloth, and crisp, starched napkins were positioned upright on the plates. Crystal goblets refracted the candlelight to shimmering effect: as a result of Peter the Great's love of European customs, the elaborate drinking vessels of silver or brass that Russians had used for centuries (the *chasha, charka, kubok,* and *stopa*) had gradually been replaced by glass goblets and shot glasses.

Faddei Bulgarin, the publisher of the conservative Saint Petersburg newspaper *The Northern Bee,* described the beauty of a mid-nineteenth-century aristocratic Russian table in a piece called "Dinner," which explained how the table should be set, with whom one should eat, and what one should eat. He insisted that the room be illuminated with beeswax candles to evoke "honey, sweet and aromatic, and the bee in meadows and flowerbeds." Gautier also took note of the Russian obsession with flowers and floral scents, complaining that Russians "live there as in a hothouse, and indeed every Russian house is a hothouse. Without, you are at the pole; within, you could fancy yourself in the tropics." In fact, the fashion for palms in the dining room, introduced midcentury under Tsar Alexander II, soon became the rage in aristocratic Saint Petersburg. Dinners in "jungles" were deemed chic, although only the truly wealthy could afford such tropical extravagance.

A love of the floral carried over to the tableware. Porcelain from both Meissen in Saxony and Sèvres in France had been fashionable in Russia since the early eighteenth century. Hoping to produce domestic porcelain of comparably high quality, Empress Elizabeth I established the Imperial Porcelain Factory in 1744; other factories followed, most notably the Gardner Factory, founded by the Englishman Francis Gardner in 1766, and the Popov Factory, founded in 1806. These Russian porcelain factories initially copied European designs but soon developed their own styles. From the time of Catherine the Great until the end of Nicholas I's reign in 1855, the Imperial Porcelain Factory produced everyday services for the royal court, in addition to the official state dinner services for which they were acclaimed. One design, called Deutsche Blumen (German Flowers), featured clusters of flowers against a white ground, with small sprigs of flowers on the rim. It proved so popular that by the 1850s naturalistic floral patterns were widespread, even among the middle class.

Wealthy Russians worked hard to create an atmosphere of enchantment for their guests. Trompe l'oeil was often part of the aesthetics. One winter evening, the acclaimed hostess Princess Zinaida Yusupova covered the entire length of her dining table with mirrored glass that encased the trunks of blossom-laden orange trees, giving the illusion of trees growing right through the table, even as snow fell outside. Imperial Russian life itself was increasingly based on expensive illusions. The aristocracy kept hothouses at enormous expense so that they could serve fruits out of season, especially pineapple, which became such a symbol of decadence that it features in Igor Severianin's famous 1915 poetry collection *Pineapples in Champagne* (*Ananasy v shampanskom*). And speaking of champagne, one of the world's greatest cuvées, Cristal from the French house of Louis Roederer, was developed expressly for Tsar Alexander II in 1876. The tsar commissioned Roederer to create the most exquisite champagne possible and further instructed that it be bottled in lead crystal, rather than in the usual dark glass, so that he could see whether the champagne had been adulterated with poison. Alexander's paranoia additionally caused him to request a flat bottom to the bottle, out of fear that a bomb could be hidden in the traditional punt, the indentation at the bottom that enables the glass to withstand the greater pressure of carbonation. His champagne precautions were ultimately for naught, as he was assassinated in 1881 by a bomb wrapped in a napkin.

Service à la Russe

In the past, Russian aristocratic banquets could last for hours and involve many different courses, as was also the practice in the rest of Europe. At medieval French banquets, cold dishes were laid out on the table, while hot dishes (more often lukewarm from sitting) were brought in from the kitchen at serving time, arrayed on large platters in the center of the table to be shared by all diners. In seventeenth-century France a new style of service—*service à la française*—became fashionable. When guests entered the banquet hall, the table was already laid in a formal pattern of dishes mandatory in both arrangement and type; diners helped themselves only to whatever was nearby. Each course often comprised dozens of dishes, and when one dish was removed, another ("the remove") immediately took its place so as not to disturb the table's artistic design.

By contrast, at a Russian-style meal, diners sat down at tables devoid of food. In medieval times, only salt, pepper, and vinegar appeared on the table, but by the nineteenth century, candelabra and lavish flower arrangements made the presentation festive. The food was served sequentially, rather than being set out all at once, and the service often became a performance, with servants parading a dramatic roast or enormous sturgeon around the table before whisking it off to the sideboard or kitchen for carving. More servants brought individual portions for each diner, a practice that entailed a huge staff—something that the upper classes freely enjoyed until the serfs were liberated in 1861. Besides requiring many bodies, Russian-style service also necessitated a vast amount of tableware. Foreign visitors accustomed to the predictability and self-containment of a French-style meal found Russian feasts confusing, since they didn't know in advance how much food would appear. The French style made it easy to pace oneself, but the Russian style delivered food hot.

Under Peter the Great, table service began to evolve toward the sequence of four courses that is familiar in Western societies today: *zakuska* (appetizer), soup, main dish, and dessert. Even though Peter mandated many changes to the table, such as allowing women to dine with men and introducing new foods, Russia's distinctive practice of sequential courses survived his reforms—a striking instance of adherence to tradition. In fact, reform worked in the other direction. Within a century *service à la russe* had taken

Western Europe by storm, despite the protests of the celebrity French chef Marie-Antoine Carême, who found it vulgar. "Is there anything more imposing than the sight of a grand table served *à la française?*" he asked. None other than Charles Dickens introduced Russian-style dining to London, and by the mid-nineteenth century, New York high society was inviting guests to dine *à la russe.* This style eventually became the norm for fashionable tables, and it is possible to trace the standard American sequence of the meal (appetizer, soup or salad, main course, and dessert) back to the practice of dining *à la russe.*

There were some variations on this pattern. An 1856 article from the journal *The Muscovite* describes the order in which a traditional Russian meal was presented, setting up a distinction between "cold" Saint Petersburg, with its French airs, and the author's beloved, generous Moscow, where meals were always "simple and hearty, like Russian hospitality." "Simple" is relative: first came a substantial appetizer (*zakuska*) course consisting of flavored vodkas and piquant small dishes, ideally presented in a separate room. The meal proper opened with soup in the dining room. Various pies, such as *kulebiaka* (fish) and *vatrushki* (farmer's cheese), were served either with or right after the soup, followed by two or three cold dishes, for instance boiled ham or galantine of pike. These cold dishes were followed in turn by two so-called sauces—hot dishes with various dressings, such as duck with mushrooms, lamb with garlic, or *poularde fricassée.* The fourth course consisted of roasts: turkey, duck, goose, pork, wildfowl, or sturgeon. In place of salad, pickles or brined (*mochonye*) lemons and apples were offered as a palate cleanser. Throughout the meal the center of the table remained empty, save for ornamentation or a dessert display, since each course was individually plated and brought in from the kitchen. Dinner edged toward conclusion with two desserts (*pirozhnye*), one "wet," the other "dry." Wet desserts, such as creams and mousses, were eaten with a spoon, while dry ones like pastries could be eaten out of hand. An assortment of kvasses, beers, and wines complemented the meal. The actual end of the meal, formally named *desert* after the French word, consisted of candies and fruits along with a variety of homemade liqueurs, cordials, ratafias, and punch. Following the practice at the royal court, mid-nineteenth-century aristocrats had beautifully designed menu cards printed to set at each place to mark special dinners.

The author of the *Muscovite* article (identified only as I.G.) waxes nostalgic for the legendary dinners of the past. Like other chroniclers, he emphasizes the surprises with which the best hosts sought to delight their guests. One particularly over-the-top meal began with a puréed soup of ruffe with burbot milt, followed by a *kulebiaka* so buttery that it melted in the mouth. Next came a turkey with truffles aromatic enough to rouse the comatose, then sturgeon à la Richelieu, its slightly sweet sauce harmonizing with the sharpness of capers and olives. The following "sauce" course consisted of sautéed poussins with champignons and scallops, and asparagus spears so large that it took only six to make up a pound. A simple salad cleansed the palate before the pièce de résistance of roast pheasant. Wondering at this point how the dessert course could possibly live up to the rest of this extraordinary meal, I.G. is confounded when a large ham is triumphantly brought in from the kitchen—something he can't possibly stomach after the roast pheasant. But it turns out that at this dinner, the food itself is illusory, rather than the setting—a brilliant example of culinary trompe l'oeil. As I.G. recounts:

Imagine my surprise: when I was served this ham, I saw that it wasn't ham after all, or salt pork, but a pastry, a most superior pastry. You see, what was it?—It was a ham, a *ham sponge cake.* The cook had taken three pink sponge layers, cut them into the shape of a ham, stacked them, and layered them with Kiev-style strawberry jam, then spread on blancmange flavored with orange flower water, ingeniously fooling the eye to look like fat on the ham, and finally, in place of the ham rind, the blancmange was frosted with a glaze of sugar and chocolate, and all of this comprised such a tasty dish that Lucullus himself wouldn't have refused it even after one of his own dinners.

Despite such culinary extravaganzas, even the most Westernized nineteenth-century menus were regularly grounded in iconic Russian dishes like kasha, sturgeon, "lazy" cabbage soup, *kulebiaka,* and other savory pies. And although champagne and imported wine flowed at fancy meals, bottles of homemade sparkling kvass (*kislye shchi*) also graced the table, the sour edge of the kvass cutting the richness of so many Frenchified dishes. Societal debates about Russia's destiny raged between the traditionalist Slavophiles and the more progressive Westernizers, but the desire for traditional foods was not a matter of nationalism or even nostalgia, since the most earthy, sharp-tasting flavors had never disappeared from the Russian table. These were simply the flavors that all Russians craved. Like the peasants who couldn't live without their lacto-fermented rye bread, the elite could not do without wild mushrooms that smelled of forest and field, brined berries that hinted of summer's sweetness, and herring that bore the sea's mineral tang. Even those who adopted French foods never lost their taste for these touchstone flavors.

Teatime

If there is one symbol of Russian hospitality beyond the traditional bread and salt, it is the samovar. Defined prosaically in the dictionary as an urn for preparing tea, the samovar is an extraordinary, not ordinary, object—decorated with medallions, gleaming in the light of a candle or lamp, smoke curling from its chimney, the water inside hissing as it boils. Samovars appear in the work of Russia's greatest writers and poets as subjects in their own right, with the ability to lift one's mood and assuage despair. The practice of drinking tea is far more recent than that of presenting bread and salt, having come to mark Russian national identity only in the nineteenth century; and yet, once tea drinking had become widespread, the phrase *chai da sakhar* (tea and sugar) became another expression for hospitality.

Tea was first introduced to Russia from China by way of Siberia. As early as 1567, emissaries from Ivan IV had spoken of this strange brew, but tea did not find its way to the royal court until 1638. Regular trade between Russia and China was established in 1689 with the signing of the Treaty of Nerchinsk. Initially Russians used tea, as they had once used vodka, for medicinal purposes, finding its high caffeine content useful in countering the effects of too much alcohol. But unlike vodka, which infiltrated all levels of society, tea remained for several centuries a luxury item, in large part due to the expense of importing it. Traveling overland from China, the early camel caravans could take eighteen months to reach Moscow. The earliest tea was transported as pressed bricks, but caravan drivers sought to ease the camels' lumpy load by conveying loose leaves in sacks. The loose tea in these sacks absorbed smoke from the nightly fires they laid en route, leading to the dark,

FIGURE 13. Unknown photographer, *On the Porch at the Dacha,* 1910s. This lively photograph communicates the relaxation and joy afforded by the dacha. The occasion is Easter, as is evident from the central plate holding the special sweet Easter bread, *kulich,* whose towering top has been sliced off and set to the side. A samovar prominently stands on the table, although alcoholic drinks likely account for the men's jovial expressions. Collection of the Multimedia Art Museum, Moscow.

smoky blend that is sold today as Russian Caravan. Later, after a large portion of the Siberian Highway had been completed in the early nineteenth century, horse-drawn sleighs carried bundles of tea that had been packed in special reed baskets lined with paper— or, for the finest tea, with lead foil, which blocked the smoke but added toxic properties not yet recognized. These bundles were then wrapped securely in leather. Much of this tea transport took place during the winter months, both because sleighs could travel quickly over the ice and because the tea was not exposed to the harmful effects of heat.

Russia was eager to develop a domestic tea industry, and yet it took several centuries to do so. Around the time of the Napoleonic Wars, the first few tea bushes were planted at the Nikitsky Botanical Garden in the far south of Crimea, not far from Yalta. But only in 1833 were attempts made to grow tea commercially, with several dozen bushes that had been smuggled in from China. The plants withered in the region's alkaline soil and dry climate, so plantations were established instead near Sukhumi on the Black Sea coast. These plantings marked the rocky beginning of Russia's domestic tea production, which came into its own only after the revolution. Tea plantations spread across Georgia, Azerbaijan, and the Krasnodar region of southern Russia, yet domestic production could not come close to meeting demand. It took a communist revolution in China and Stalin's personal intervention with Mao Zedong to ensure a steady supply of tea from China—and then it was secured only as part of an agreement extending Soviet credit as well as equipment and technology to the Chinese.

By the early nineteenth century tea had become a near fetish among Moscow's aristocracy and wealthy merchants. They stored valuable loose-leaf tea in beautifully crafted boxes, complete with locks, and served it from elegant tea services made by the finest porcelain manufacturers. By midcentury, tea drinking had spread to the less affluent segments of society, for whom owning a samovar was a source of pride. On his 1839 visit to Russia, the French aristocrat Marquis Astolphe de Custine wrote with considerable disdain about the Russian peasants, their customs, and their houses. He did, however, approve of their tea:

On the table shines a brass samovar and a teapot. The tea is always of good quality, made with care, and if one doesn't want to drink it in its pure form, good milk can be found everywhere. This elegant beverage served in hovels furnished like barns—I say barns to express myself politely—reminds me of the [hot] chocolate of the Spaniards. (Marquis de Custine, *La Russie en 1839*)

Perhaps because of the huge increase in tea consumption, temperance societies and religious figures like the revered monastic priest Serafim Sarovsky (later canonized as a saint) denounced tea as a dangerous, even demonic, substance, and one that threatened to bankrupt the country. The imprecations against tea were directed not only against its supposed deleterious effects on health, morals, and the economy; they also evinced xenophobic sentiment against the Chinese, arising from a widespread fear of Chinese expansion into the territories of the Russian far east. (In fact, over the course of the nineteenth century, the opposite happened: Russia expanded ever farther eastward, gaining the Amur and Ussuri River basins in the 1860 Treaty of Peking.)

Nevertheless, tea boomed, and the fashion—and passion—for drinking it led to the rise of the samovar industry, which was concentrated in Tula, a city south of Moscow that was already the center of arms manufacture and metallurgy. The first samovar workshop was organized in 1778; by 1850, the city had twenty-eight samovar factories that produced over one hundred thousand samovars a year.

The origins of the samovar's design are murky, and it is unclear whether this vessel arrived in Russia from the East or the West. The model may have been the Mongolian hot pot or the elaborate Dutch urns that had taps rather than spouts. Or perhaps its forerunners were Byzantine urns or European fountains for cooling wine. Whatever its origin, the Russians adapted a foreign receptacle into a useful object that became not only very much their own, but one that epitomizes Russianness. The oldest Russian-made samovars were fabricated like the portable kettles that had long been used to dispense *sbiten*, the hot, spiced honey drink. These early samovars had long, curved spouts rather than the angular spigot that later became standard.

Samovars were crafted for all sorts of uses: a small number were even fashioned with interior strainers for making coffee, though this style is found today only in a few remote parts of the Russian north, where coffee was introduced via Siberia's network of rivers. Samovar sizes ranged from sixteen-gallon urns for use in public venues to tiny, individual models jocularly known as "samovar-egoists" or "bachelor's delight." Special traveling sets were fashionable among the leisured classes, who took them on picnics and journeys, accompanied by elaborate hampers outfitted with a teapot, glasses or cups and saucers, spoons, a tea caddy, matches, containers for milk, sugar, and jam, and sometimes a flagon of cognac or rum—and, of course, a platoon of servants to tote it all.

The body of the samovar contains a central cylinder that is filled with fuel—charcoal, kindling, pine cones, or hot coals plucked from the masonry stove. Water is poured into the vessel surrounding the cylinder, and it heats up quickly. If the samovar has a design defect, it's that the burning fuel produces smoke. Outdoors, that isn't a problem, but indoors, the smoke hangs in the air unless the samovar is fitted with a metal venting pipe. Well-to-do families connected this small pipe to the stove, which carried the smoke into the flue and out of the house. Peasants who could afford this refinement lived in so-called "white" cottages and were a lot healthier than those who lived in sooty, fume-filled "black" cottages—unfortunately the majority of the peasant population. Even so, the samovar represented such an object of prestige that people continued to use it even when smoke settled in the air.

The tea itself is brewed into a very strong concentrate (*zavarka*) in a small teapot that sits within a ring atop the urn. This *zavarka* is poured into cups or glasses, with hot water added from the samovar according to each person's taste. Nineteenth-century protocol had ladies drinking tea from fine porcelain cups, while fashionable men drank it from faceted glasses inserted into metal holders called *podstakanniki*. Merchants usually drank their tea from deep saucers, the advantage being that the saucer's broad surface cooled the liquid quickly. For this technique a little agility was required. The tea drinker balanced the saucer on all five fingers, a position that necessitated slurping. This noisy intake was part of the pleasure of drinking the tea, though the aristocracy disdained this practice. Tea drinking, though frequent and commonplace, was at the same time ritualized, with particular codes of behavior for each level of society.

Nearly all Russians, no matter their standing, liked to sweeten their tea with sugar. Sugar was chipped from large, solid cones into irregular, bite-sized lumps that were most often clenched between the teeth as the tea was sipped. Because the sugar was dense and hard—not like today's highly refined cubes—it melted slowly, and a single lump could last for ten cups (or saucers) of tea. The sensation of drinking tea through sugar (*vprikusku*) is delightful, if bad for the teeth. Of course tea can also be drunk *vnakladku*—with the lump of sugar dropped right into the cup or glass, though this use was considered extravagant, given sugar's expense until the late nineteenth century. Those who were strapped for resources were reputed to drink their tea *vprigliadku,* without any sugar, while gazing at a precious lump as they drank, as if to summon the experience of sweetness.

No matter how sugar is used, tea is always served with other sweeteners, often honey or syrupy jam, which are placed in small dishes called *rozetki.* Lemon and milk can also be offered. Drinking tea is a social rite, an occasion to gather and talk, often for hours, while enjoying delicacies like fresh fruit, buns, and pies sweet and savory. The pies themselves are often highly ornamental, sealed by means of decorative pleating, their crusts covered with scraps of dough shaped into leaves, flowers, and other organic or geometric forms in bas-relief. For a golden sheen, the crust is usually glazed with an egg wash before baking. No wonder the Russians say, "The beauty of a house lies not in its walls, but in its pies."

Hospitality under Duress

After the revolution, the huge influx of people into Moscow and Petrograd (Saint Petersburg) caused dire housing shortages. The communal apartments created in response necessitated sharing a kitchen with strangers, an arrangement that threatened the norms of family life. That threat didn't concern Soviet social theorists, who questioned the very premise of private life and the nuclear family. They sought instead to create a new environment, a new everyday life, or *novyi byt,* that would transform people into model Soviet citizens. Idealistic architects, taking a cue from the ultra-efficient Frankfurt Kitchen designed by the Austrian architect Margarete Schütte-Lihotzky in 1926, envisioned new types of dwellings. They designed buildings with individual apartments sharing access to central spaces, including a kitchen, a dining hall, a nursery, a gym, and a laundry. These apartments varied in layout and size, though none included space for family dining. Standard apartments had a kitchenette only about eight feet square, while the smallest ones, the so-called living cells, had no kitchens at all (unhappy residents were known to smuggle in hot plates). Although most of these projects were never realized, in 1930 the architect Moisei Ginzburg and his student Ignaty Milinis built the Narkomfin House in Moscow, intended to steer its inhabitants toward a new, collective way of life. The communal spaces were supposed to liberate women from domestic chores—or, as Ginzburg put it in his book *Dwelling,* to "facilitate a rapid and painless transition to higher social forms of housekeeping." Though the building, which still stands, remains a prime example of visionary Constructivist architecture, the mode of life it prescribed was neither popular nor practicable, and by the mid-1930s, the government once again recognized the nuclear family as a viable unit.

Food for Russians has meaning only when it is shared, and even the smallest pleasures can become occasions for celebration. But in the twentieth century the tradition of hospitality was strained by far more than a communal ideology. In Leningrad during the siege, sharing was nearly impossible, because one's very life depended on a tiny ration of bread. The loss of hospitality represented a particularly debasing aspect of life during the siege: it contributed to a sense of existing only in one's body, even as the body itself had become alien and strange through wasting away from hunger. Even so, when there was strength enough, people engaged in small celebrations. The ballerina Vera Kostrovitskaia, in her unpublished memoirs, relates how Kira, a young hospital worker, sprinkled tiny squares of bread with a bit of hoarded sugar to treat her colleagues to "blockade pastries."

The urge to share one's table, no matter how meager, is a national trait that endures despite wars and political upheavals that create desperate shortages. Even during the worst periods of scarcity in the USSR, people pulled out all the stops to gather and celebrate special occasions. This is why, in post-Soviet Russia, when the economy crashed and inflation skyrocketed in 1998, the Russians' sense of identity was shaken. Ordinary people couldn't offer guests a proper meal. The inability to extend hospitality wasn't just a matter of being unable to entertain: it went to the heart of what it means to be Russian. Russians are deeply social, and their historical isolation, due to extreme weather and often impassable roads, made them all the more eager for company.

This national longing for conviviality is captured by a popular joke from the Soviet era. Three men are stranded on a desert island—an American, a Frenchman, and a Russian—with nothing other than a case of beer and a deck of cards. They're drinking beer and playing cards when out of a bottle a genie appears. He offers them each one wish. The American goes first. "I gotta get back to New York," he says. "My partner's probably swindling me!" In an instant, he's gone. Next the Frenchman cries, "Oh, I must return to Paris, tout de suite, or my mistress will find another man!" He disappears instantaneously, too. The Russian is left alone on the island. He hangs his head. "It was so nice," he mourns. "We had lots of beer to drink, games, and friendship . . . Bring them back!"

Coda

Post-Soviet Russia

The collapse of the line was much more painful for the collective Soviet body than the collapse of the Soviet Union. With the loss of the queue the people lost an important therapeutic ritual of self-acknowledgment which had been honed and polished over the course of decades and had become a daily necessity, like drugs for an addict. Then, suddenly, there were no drugs.

VLADIMIR SOROKIN, "Farewell to the Queue"
(trans. Jamey Gambrell)

The fall of the Soviet Union cannot be blamed on the opening of McDonald's near Red Square in Moscow on January 31, 1990, but the fast-food chain did make a crack in the Iron Curtain. Nearly two years would pass before the Soviet Union collapsed, in December 1991, but the introduction of American fast food ushered in a sea change in public dining in Russia. During the Soviet years standards had deteriorated to the point where rude doormen, surly service, and unclean conditions were the norm. Suddenly, here was a restaurant where everything on the menu was always available, quality was controlled, tables sparkled, and the service was both quick and friendly. On opening day, over thirty thousand people showed up to taste American burgers. Police arrived to con-

FIGURE 14. Alexander Steshanov, *Queue at McDonald's*, Moscow, 1990. The opening of the USSR's first McDonald's was a seminal moment in Russian history. Crowd control had to be instituted for the tens of thousands of people who showed up to get a taste of the famous American burger. Note the sign with the Soviet star and the Communist hammer and sickle affixed to the bottom of the McDonald's logo with its golden arches. Collection of the Multimedia Art Museum, Moscow.

trol the exuberant crowd, though no police were needed. People stood patiently in the cold, in a line that stretched for kilometers.

With nine hundred seats, the Moscow McDonald's was the largest in the world. So excited were the restaurant's early patrons by the novelty of all they encountered that they saved the disposable takeout boxes and cups to reuse at home. Many experienced the restaurant as a sort of liberation. As one customer later reported to the Voice of America, "I felt like I was eating America itself." Store shelves may have been empty of food, but McDonald's, like a magical shop in a fairy tale, always replenished itself.

The extraordinary success of McDonald's in Russia has less to do with its American identity than with the way the corporation anticipated and advanced the country's radical transition from a centralized economy to a free-market one. With the collapse of the Soviet Union, foreign consultants like Jeffrey Sachs advocated "shock therapy," seeking to rapidly liberalize trade, privatize holdings, and make Russia both financially stable and competitive in the global marketplace. These structural changes were ultimately derailed by back-room deals between the government and the new class of oligarchs, who exploited Russia's riches and left the economy in a shambles. But McDonald's followed its own path. From the start, the corporation set up a manufacturing arm outside Moscow to ensure an uninterrupted supply of high-quality meat and produce (the locals called the facility "McGulag" because of the barbed wire surrounding it). Initially, roughly 80 percent of the ingredients for McDonald's offerings had to be imported, but the company strove to encourage private enterprise and local suppliers. By late 2020, 98 percent of the corporation's supplies were provided by domestic companies that served 750 McDonald's outlets spread across the vast expanse of Russia.

The fast-food chain's presence has not been without controversy. In 2014, after McDonald's closed its three outlets in Crimea following Russia's forcible annexation of the region, the right-wing politician Vladimir Zhirinovsky called for booting the company out of Russia altogether, explicitly linking nationalist politics and food choices. That link was even more evident in an incident from 2012, when a woman allegedly discovered worms in a McDonald's burger she bought in Moscow. This news report provoked outrage. Russia's chief medical doctor, Gennady Onishchenko, weighed in with these words: "I remind our fellow citizens that hamburgers, even without worms, are not a proper nutritional choice for the populace of Moscow and Russia. This food is not ours." The word "ours" (*nash*) carries meanings both overtly political (the erstwhile youth movement "Ours" was closely allied with the Kremlin) and emotional, harking back to Prince Mikhail Shcherbatov's impassioned eighteenth-century diatribe against the use of foreign ingredients. Most telling of all, Onishchenko referred to the hamburgers as *eda*, not *pishcha*, his word choice signaling their inability to provide either physical or emotional nourishment.

A New Restaurant Landscape

McDonald's is now a fixture in Russia, but its success should be weighed in more than strictly financial terms. Although there is much to criticize in the corporation's model of cheap, unhealthy food and low wages, not to mention its role in spreading American fast-food culture across the globe, McDonald's was good for Russia. "Service with a smile" may be a cliché, but its introduction into a country where boorish treatment by the staff was the norm proved galvanizing, even revolutionary. Today, good service is not only widespread in Russia, it is also expected, as are clean surroundings, and McDonald's outsize role in promoting these conditions deserves to be recognized.

The company's success was not effortless. In fact, it wasn't the first American fast-food endeavor in Moscow. In April 1988 the visionary American entrepreneur Louis Piancone Sr. took advantage of Mikhail Gorbachev's relaxed policies under perestroika to open Astro Pizza, a large, shiny GMC food truck that dispensed freshly made pizza for only 1.75 rubles a slice. Sporting a sign with Russian and American flags, the truck would pop up in various

FIGURE 15. Yuri Abramochkin, *Queuing for American Astro Pizza in Downtown Moscow,* 1988. The Astro Pizza food truck was a huge hit with Muscovites, and its owner, Louis Piancone Sr., looked forward to experimenting with new toppings. As he told the *Los Angeles Times,* "If caviar's what they want, that's what we'll give them. A little variation will be good." Sadly, his venture proved short-lived. Logistical problems with currency conversion and the sourcing of ingredients forced Astro Pizza to close after only a few months. Sputnik Images.

locations around the city, keeping its fans guessing where it might next appear. Yet despite its popularity, Astro Pizza closed after only six months. Piancone had been more interested in the optics of cultural exchange than in the business end of his project, and he hadn't foreseen the difficulties of operating in the Russian market, without convertible currency.

The arrival of American food signaled a new phase in the Soviet government's receptiveness to foreign investment. The ascent of McDonald's led other American fast-food chains to open outlets in Russia. Pizza Hut arrived in 1990, a few months after McDonald's.

Like McDonald's, Pizza Hut's Moscow outlet became the company's highest-volume store worldwide, and not only because it catered to local tastes with a "Moskva" pizza topped with sardines, tuna, mackerel, salmon, and onion. As the Russian economy worsened, however, the company faltered. Pizza Hut hoped to turn its poor performance around with a television commercial, as it had successfully done in the US in 1995, when it enlisted Donald Trump and his erstwhile wife Ivana to boost the disappointing sales of the company's new stuffed-crust pizza. Thus in 1997 Pizza Hut convinced Mikhail Gorbachev to appear with his granddaughter in a commercial for Russian television. In the sixty-second clip, a multigenerational family at a nearby table argues about Gorbachev's legacy—did he give Russia freedom and opportunity or political and economic instability? The question remains unanswered until the peacemaking matriarch declares, "Because of him, we have Pizza Hut!" Then the entire restaurant rises to toast Gorbachev. But unlike Trump's cameo appearance, Gorbachev's failed, and Pizza Hut pulled out of the Moscow market in 1998. (Under Vladimir Putin, it returned.)

Meanwhile, the rapid proliferation of other American chains, including Dunkin' Donuts and Baskin-Robbins, led Russian entrepreneurs to open chains of their own. Many of these new ventures based their appeal on pride in Russian food, as opposed to American imports. The first to appear was Russian Bistro, in 1995, with strong support from Moscow's then-mayor, Yuri Luzhkov. The menu, touted as offering authentically Russian and high-quality fast food, featured a variety of inexpensive savory pies as well as *pel'meni*. But the chain expanded too quickly and ultimately failed, as did the blini chain BlinDonald's. More successful was Teremok, which opened in 1998 and is still in operation. Originally a chain of blini kiosks, it now has hundreds of outlets throughout Russia, including some sit-down restaurants. Teremok has recently rebranded itself as "not fast food," emphasizing instead "a contemporary approach in which outstanding taste and quick service unite." Nevertheless, McDonald's, Burger King, and KFC continue to dominate Russia's fast-food scene.

The desire to announce Russian identity through cuisine is also evident in the higher-end restaurants that opened in Moscow during the early post-Soviet years, their names trumpeting Russia's cultural past. Few restaurants in New York, London, or Paris are named after literary, artistic, or historical figures, but Moscow's culturally themed restaurants include Yermak, Pushkin, Oblomov, Evenings on a Farm (named after a Gogol story), Petrov-Vodkin, White Sun of the Desert and Prisoner of the Caucasus (both named after Soviet cult films), and Petrovich (named after a Soviet cartoon character), as well as the more recently opened Grand Café Dr. Zhivago. In this way Moscow's restaurants are implicit reminders of the country's cultural heritage, a commercial branding of the Russian patrimony.

These restaurants are more notable for their decor than for the excellence of their food, a phenomenon that connects them to Russia's long-standing love of illusion. In the early post-Soviet days, going out to eat at such themed restaurants offered an escape from the drudgery of daily life, whether in the nineteenth-century interior of Café Pushkin or the Central Asian ambience of White Sun of the Desert. The city's most talked-about restaurants aimed to stage a meal, not just serve one. To visit a trendy restaurant was to enter a fantasyland and leave reality behind, turning each venue into a virtual "theater of consumption." The mega-restaurateur Andrei Dellos, whose Café Pushkin and restaurant Turandot remain two of the most glamorous and (literally) fantastic spots in Moscow, has claimed that after seventy-odd years of Soviet rule, the "Russians [were] tired of ideology, and my goal is to give people somewhere they can come, enjoy themselves, and dream."

This escape into dream is most palpable at Dellos's extravagant Turandot, which rivals the profligacy of prerevolutionary times. Opened in December 2005, Turandot occupies 65,000 square feet in a $50 million re-creation of a rococo palace. Dellos devoted six years to building and outfitting Turandot. He tore down a neoclassical ensemble of eighteenth- and nineteenth-century mansions (one of which had belonged to a lover of Catherine the Great) and hired lighting and set designers from the Bolshoi Theater. Guests enter the restaurant through a Florentine courtyard replete with genuine eighteenth-century Venetian lanterns and a Buccellati showroom selling exquisite jewelry for tens of thousands of rubles. The restaurant's central hall features a two-story rotunda with a chandelier of gilded iron bearing pendants of crystal, quartz, and amethyst from the Urals, Brazil, and Madagascar. No detail was overlooked or underwrought—even the toilets are crafted of Delft porcelain. As for the food, there are no herring cheeks, but in its early days the menu featured a rare turtle consommé. Today the food is much more generic, with sushi, spring rolls, fried rice, and other "pan-Asian" dishes incongruously served in this opulent setting.

At the other extreme lies nostalgia for Soviet-era dining. Petrovich, with its kitschy decor, entered early into the game, but others followed, such as Stolovaya 57 in the GUM department store, which turned the concept of a workers' cafeteria into something trendy. As a *New York Times* article put it in 2019, "The longing for service without a smile is part of a general nostalgia in

Russia." An important aspect of Soviet restaurant life was the exclusivity maintained by doormen who would not allow ordinary people into the few good restaurants that existed. A sign stating "No seats available" hung on most doors, although the doormen could usually be bribed. Keeping people out took on the different form of "face control" in the early post-Soviet years, when doormen sized up the look of the person desiring to see and be seen. Today eating out has become normalized, and entry to any given restaurant is more a question of affordability or of snagging a reservation. Where the Soviet system had positioned restaurants as an indulgence for special occasions, people now eat out simply for pleasure on ordinary days. This shift demanded a new ideological framework that sanctions engaging in epicurean activity for its own sake. And in the thirty years since the Soviet Union collapsed, many diners have also educated themselves. Having tasted foreign food, they are more sophisticated, with higher standards. Moscow and Saint Petersburg remain at the cutting edge of culinary fashion, but cities throughout Russia have restaurants and cafés that specialize in Italian, Japanese, Thai, Vietnamese, Georgian, and other cuisines.

And burgers are back. In 2015 another restaurant titan, Arkady Novikov, opened the burger chain Farsh (Ground Beef), which soon gained a following for its well-marbled Black Angus beef patties and airy potato buns. Novikov hired the French chef Kamel Benmamar, who had worked at Michelin-starred restaurants in France and London, to create what he bills as "craft fast food." A year later the restaurateur Yuri Levitas partnered with the controversial hip-hop artist Timati (Timur Yunusov) to open the Black Star Burger chain, named after Timati's recording label. The chain includes dozens of restaurants and franchises across Russia and the former Soviet Union. Like the burgers at Farsh, Black Star's are juicy, so much so that each order comes with a pair of hypoallergenic, recyclable, black nitrile gloves for eating the messy burgers without dirtying one's hands. The black gloves became so trendy that burger joints throughout Russia now regularly offer them. The burger-centric blog Burger House has called Black Star Burger "the first Russian national burger," which may not be far off the mark, since Timati openly supports Putin and Moscow's pro-Kremlin mayor, Sergei Sobyanin. Even the Chechen strongman Ramzan Kadyrov has given the burgers a thumbs-up in an Instagram video. It would seem that in the thirty years since McDonald's first opened in Moscow, burgers have come full circle: Black Star Burger has traversed the globe to open an outlet on hipster Fairfax Avenue in Los Angeles, while across the country, in Brooklyn's Russian neighborhood of Brighton Beach, black gloves are now de rigueur with burger orders. As one café owner explained, "It's awesome to sit here, in gloves, eat burgers, see all this and be seen. You feel like you're in Moscow."

Shock Waves and Subsistence

The excesses of fashionable dining are concentrated in Moscow. Elsewhere, many people can barely make ends meet, so even though restaurants abound, not everyone can afford to patronize them. Russians, particularly of the older generation, have suffered psychic scarring from the economic chaos of the immediate post-Soviet period. Inflation rose to over 2,000 percent in 1992, and in the mid-1990s the nation's economic output was about half what it had been in 1989. Between 1990 and 1994 male life expectancy dropped from 63.8 years to a shocking 57.7. Salaries often went unpaid for months, and food prices were high. The Soviet safety net had disappeared, and basic survival seemed threatened, especially for those living on minuscule pensions. The value of the ruble kept diminishing until its utter collapse in 1998, when the government devalued the currency so sharply that one thousand old rubles equaled only one new one, wiping out people's savings.

In the late Soviet years, people had endured shortages and at times been hungry, but the 1990s brought true desperation. Having experienced famine within their collective memory, as well as relentless propaganda about the cruelty and hunger suffered under capitalist systems, Russians felt deep anxiety. They found some relief by turning once again to the informal exchange networks that provided a critical alternative to inadequate government provisioning, and they also turned to their dacha gardens. Private possession of garden plots had been legalized with the collapse of the Soviet Union, and owners were allowed to expand beyond the previous limit of six *sotka*s. People began to feed themselves. Potatoes, in particular, represented security and well-being, though other vegetables and fruits were grown as well. As reported by the United Nations Development Programme, approximately 65 percent of families in Moscow were making use of garden plots in 1991. Self-sufficiency was even more crucial in rural areas, where virtually no outside food was available. Tellingly, the Russian term for this kind of subsistence farming is *natural'noe sel'skoe khoziaistvo*, or "natural agriculture." Cultivating a kitchen garden is nothing new; it is a continuation of the way Russians have survived for over a thousand years.

There is more to the dacha gardens than alleviating shortages. Not all food is created equal. Russians, like others, believe that food grown by one's own labors, on a familiar plot of land, is both tastier and healthier than food from other sources. And usually they are right. But at issue are questions not just of quality or self-reliance but also of connectedness to the land, to the soil. This attitude is tied up with long-standing beliefs about the spiritual benefits that nature, and by extension working the land, can bestow. Cultivating a dacha garden represents more than a response to exigency or an urge for a hobby: it is a key cultural activity that has its roots in the very word *dacha,* which stems from the morpheme "to give." When weekend gardeners have surplus produce, they rarely bring it to market to sell but prefer to share it with family and friends.

This cultural trait explains why people continued to cultivate dacha gardens even after the economy stabilized, spending back-breaking hours tending their plots when they could easily afford to buy all the food that they needed. To its credit, Russia's legislative body, the Duma, in 2003 passed the Private Garden Plot Act, which offered small private plots for free. (It was, of course, in the government's interest to encourage this small-scale farming to offset its own agricultural failures.) As recently as 2004, smallholder plots produced 51 percent of Russia's total agricultural output, largely in fruits and vegetables. But the real benefit was less economic than spiritual. Russians retain a love of the land; they like to dig in the soil and cultivate orchards.

The production from small, private plots has fallen off over the past fifteen years, but dacha gardens are still widely tended, even if they are more of a talisman and a source of psychological and physical well-being than an urgent response to food shortages. There is also a generational shift: young people may have demanding jobs that don't allow them to put in the time or effort it takes to cultivate sustainable gardens, or they simply choose not to. Thus labor-intensive potato beds have given way to decorative flowerbeds, though the potato retains its hold on the Russian psyche, if only for reasons of nostalgia. The village of Norenskaya in Russia's far north, where the poet Joseph Brodsky was exiled, is now virtually deserted. Yet hundreds of people flock there each September to participate in a festival called The Poetic Potato. The genesis of this celebration lies in the last moments of Brodsky's exile, before international pressure forced his release on September 23, 1965. As he was led from his lodgings, his landlady allegedly called after him: "But how am I going to dig the potatoes myself?" At which Brodsky promised he would return to help. (He never did; he was expelled from the Soviet Union in 1972.) The festival was inaugurated in 2016, on the seventy-fifth anniversary of Brodsky's birth. Participants of all ages gather to dig, cook, and eat the annual crop. They also read and discuss Brodsky's poetry. Some take the odd potato home to cultivate their own crop for the following year, symbolically seeding the poet's verses throughout the country.

Healthy in Spirit and Body

The injunction to be healthy in both mind and body, common in Western cultures, dates back to the ancient Greeks. Russians, though, construe this mandate as being healthy in *spirit* and body (*i dushoi i telom*). Being close to nature—through farming or foraging or simply taking in fresh air with a walk in the park—is a means of achieving this harmony. How one acquires food is also important, with informal networks considered more reliable and better for body and spirit than the anonymous food chain. If you cannot grow your own food, next best is getting it from someone familiar, whether that be a family friend, a distant acquaintance, or a customary merchant. Russians believe that the giver's or seller's positive attributes enhance the taste of the food they provide. The people in their networks further embody the concept of *ours,* which can be understood in terms of personal relationships as well as on a more political, even nationalist level—a point of pride that became especially salient after the 2014 sanctions that were imposed by Western nations following Russia's annexation of Crimea.

Yet even within a nationalist framework, not every agricultural product is good, even if it is "ours." Revelations of the environmental disasters that occurred during the Soviet years—desertification, soil contaminated with heavy metals, disastrous pollution from fertilizer runoff—has led consumers to seek out "ecologically clean" produce (*ekologicheski chistye produkty*), a term that embraces not just organic farming practices but also an identifiable human source in the chain of production. With less time to grow, preserve, and cook their own food, city dwellers are ever more concerned with the provenance of the food they buy. They have embraced the buzzwords of local and organic, non-GMO, vegan, and gluten-free, even for products like kasha that have almost always met these criteria.

Another indicator of the demand for wholesomeness can be seen in the success of the organic grocery chain VkusVill (Tasteville), which touts itself as "a grocery store for healthy eating." This home-grown chain began in 2009 with a small store called the Little Cottage that offered farm-fresh dairy products. By 2011 this single store had grown to eighty, and in 2012 the first Tasteville opened, selling many other products besides dairy, sourced directly from the producers. The company now has over one thousand stores, in which 95 percent of the products bear the store's private label. This focus on local production proved visionary, particularly during the chaos that ensued after sanctions were imposed and the ruble once again plunged along with oil prices. Tasteville flourished, offering discounts even as food prices skyrocketed in other stores. The company has continued to expand, in recent years adding numerous local mini-markets, kiosks, and even vending machines so that people can eat healthily away from home. Not even the COVID-19 pandemic slowed the chain down; they quickly instituted a website to allow contactless shopping, and customers could also track store specials on a smartphone app. Yet even with a digital interface, Tasteville has managed to promote a sense of the human dimension that is so important to the Russian understanding of eating well, thanks to its friendly messaging, extraordinary customer service, and commitment to social values. Here, in a country only thirty years removed from the dysfunctional Soviet model of provisioning, such a consumer-oriented approach is truly notable. As Tasteville's website proclaims, "We confer positive emotions."

Positive emotions have rarely been the goal of Russian directives about proper nutrition and health. The Soviets made nutrition and hygiene a state-sponsored priority—the title of the Soviet culinary bible, *The Book of Tasty and Healthy Food,* is not accidental. But for many Soviet citizens, the book's recipes remained aspirational, its prescriptions impossible to follow, when protein- and vitamin-rich foods were in such short supply. In post-Soviet Russia, an increasing number of consumers have become vigilant about their own and their family's health, and as of 2018, overall life expectancy had risen to nearly 73 from its early post-Soviet nadir. But because not everyone has had the means or the desire to eat healthily, the government decided to intervene. Russia's Federal Service for Surveillance of Consumer Rights Protection and Human Well-

Being put new regulations in place for school lunches beginning January 1, 2021. All pupils must be served hot lunches, with iodized salt used in the kitchen to encourage cognitive development. Fatty liverwurst is verboten, as is the child-friendly navy-style macaroni that was a Soviet favorite. (This calorific dish of macaroni mixed with pan-fried onions and ground beef was once served instead of the usual buckwheat porridge to reward sailors for an especially hard day of stoking the ship's boiler.) The commission also suggests substituting venison or horsemeat for beef, since they are lower in saturated fats. All of these measures are good. But other diktats outlaw foods that are deeply rooted in Russian culinary culture, such as mushrooms, *kholodets* (meat aspic), herring *forshmak* (minced herring and onions, often with mashed potatoes), and the vegetable soup known as *okroshka* (perhaps because it calls for forbidden kvass, which is lightly alcoholic, or because it is cold). Most startling of all is the catalog of proscribed condiments, including the vinegar, horseradish, and mustard that have long defined the Russian table. To rear a generation of children on bland food is not only culturally inappropriate but also misguided.

While navigating the complexities of modern life, Russians find that they have less time for certain pursuits that they enjoyed in the past, such as putting up mountains of preserves or regularly steaming in the *banya*. Yet even today, Russians insist on the shared table as essential to physical and spiritual health. Eating together, whether at home or beyond, remains an important aspect of Russian life. Sitting and chatting over pastries and tea, raising vodka toasts over salty *zakuski*, sharing steaming bowls of *pel'meni*—these acts of conviviality enable a momentary suspension of modern time pressure and an uplifting communion with others.

Reclaiming the Past

The concern with food that is "ours" embraces not only healthy eating but also a desire to resurrect Russia's culinary heritage, much of which was lost during the Soviet years. This desire to reclaim the past is not a strictly post-Soviet phenomenon. In fact, one of the earliest cookbooks ever published in Russia, the 1816 *The Russian Kitchen, or Instructions for Making All Sorts of Real Russian Dishes and for Putting Up Various Preserves,* rues the loss of a national cuisine, reflecting a fear that the "genuine" Russian way of preparing food was disappearing under assault from the many foreign dishes and methods that had been introduced over the past decades. Not incidentally, this cookbook by Vasily Levshin coincided with the rise in nationalism after the stunning defeat of Napoleon's Russian campaign. Levshin advocates a return to the "simple" national dishes that had increasingly given way to "foreign, complicated" dishes with their multitude of seasonings that he considered not only unnatural for Russians but also harmful to their health.

The backlash against gastronomic incursions from the West in the post-Soviet years was not immediate. With the lifting of restrictions on imported foods, Russians thrilled to all things foreign, eager to experience a completely new range of foods and tastes. Foreign foods enjoyed a cachet that native ones did not. Consumers who could afford it even preferred Swedish Absolut to domestic brands of vodka. (Although Absolut regularly scores high in British and American blind tastings, the desire for such insipid vodka points to a different motivation in Russia.) Where salad had once almost invariably meant a composed dish of cooked, dressed vegetables, sometimes with the addition of meat or fish, young people turned to leafy green salads. Most strikingly, springy baguettes made from wheat flour were prized over Russia's traditional, dense sourdough rye. Restaurants and cafés offering a wide variety of global foods proliferated. Sushi, in particular, became so ubiquitous that it was served virtually everywhere, even in expensive Italian restaurants. The overarching desire for the new and "exotic" overshadowed the fact that Russia has long had its own version of sashimi in the form of *stroganina,* thinly shaved slices of raw, frozen whitefish.

Novel foods led to experiments like an early post-Soviet pizza with sardines and sliced kiwis, though the combination is perhaps no more unusual than "Hawaiian" pizza with ham and pineapples. In some cases, unfamiliar imports led to poignant, even comedic moments, as when American bright red plastic Solo cups became inexplicably chic. Not realizing that the cups are intended for cold drinks, people set them out next to samovars holding hot water for tea, discovering too late that the cups would melt and then collapse on contact with hot water.

In the new millennium the unqualified embrace of foreign foods began to diminish. Leading the charge against them was a young man named Boris Akimov, who in 2009 created an organization called LavkaLavka (ShopShop), which aimed to instill pride in Russia's own produce and in its age-old methods of preservation and preparation. Akimov initially focused on the country's small farms. Over one hundred million acres of farmland had fallen out of production in the first two decades after the Soviet Union's collapse. Fields on abandoned collective farms had been overrun by weeds, and farm buildings had fallen into disrepair. A vast amount of arable land lay fallow. Akimov wanted to promote sustainable farming methods and offer a retail outlet for small-scale farmers' crops. At the same time he hoped to revitalize the countryside, whose villages had emptied out when people gained the freedom to move to the cities. His project gradually evolved into a farmers' cooperative with a presence in Moscow and Saint Petersburg that includes farm-to-table cafés as well as shops. The company's success, however, was secured by the 2014 sanctions, which forced Russia to turn to its own supply chain once thousands of products could no longer be imported. For instance, one large grocery chain, Azbuka Vkusa (Alphabet of Taste), had carried over 350 imported cheeses before the embargo. When the chain suddenly had to turn to domestic production, it created a new demand for local products. LavkaLavka was poised to jump right into the market, and business boomed. The company remains steadfast in its commitment to quality. All of the cheeses it sells are made with milk, not the palm oil that Russian corporate manufacturers often substitute in order to make inexpensive cheese.

In valorizing native produce over imports, the sanctions prompted a major shift in public attitudes. Young Russians, once cut off from traditional practices, have been actively working to uncover and revive old ways. A new generation of artisans, keen to recover a culture that was stolen during the Soviet years, is planting heritage crops, gathering wild foods for pleasure, and making ancient craft foods like *tolokno* (toasted oat flour) and forgotten drinks like *beryozovitsa,* lightly fermented birch sap. The presentation of these foods reveals a sophisticated awareness of global culinary trends. Along with the classic "twenty-four-hour" cabbage soup simmered slowly in a masonry stove, LavkaLavka's café menu offers such dishes as whitefish (*muksun*) from Siberia's Lena River, served with marinated onions, cornelian cherry juice, and rye croutons; duck pâté on spelt bread with onion jam and redcurrant sauce; and venison tartare with porcini pâté, salted egg yolk, and alfalfa.

This activity carries more than a tinge of nationalist sentiment, especially given the renewed political tensions with the West. The debate that was famously played out over dinner in Tolstoy's *Anna Karenina* over a hundred years ago—between virtuous home-style cabbage soup and kasha, and decadent foreign imports like Flensburg oysters, Parmesan cheese, and French Chablis—once again has currency. The Chelyabinsk chef Maxim Syrnikov has found a wide audience for his cookbooks like *Real Russian Food* and *Real Russian Holidays,* which describe age-old methods and recipes for bygone dishes in language that captures the vocabulary and cadences of folk speech. He teaches readers how to prepare numerous old-fashioned porridges, such as "green kasha," made from unripe rye that is baked slowly with milk in a masonry stove; and *kulaga,* made from malted, slightly fermented rye that is baked into a firm mass that takes on the intrinsic sweetness of the malt. Syrnikov's books are significant not just for their documentation of Russian foodways but also for the connoisseurship he discloses. Russian peasants treated the lowliest vegetables in ways that reveal how deeply they understood the limited ingredients they had to work with. For instance, the most subtly flavored sauerkraut, called *kroshevo,* requires great attentiveness in a process that involves more than simple salting. *Kroshevo* is made not from the inner leaves of the cabbage, as standard sauerkraut is, but from the second and third layers of leaves (the outermost, coarse "gray" leaves are handled differently). Boiling water is poured over the chopped leaves, which are then covered and left to steam for a couple of days. They are then massaged vigorously against the bottom of the barrel and left to ferment for another day, after which the

massaging is repeated. On the fourth day the cabbage is transferred to a barrel containing a weak (2 percent) brine. In a similarly
laborious process, spicy black radish is turned into a once-beloved
dessert called *mazunia,* made by dehydrating the sliced radish,
then pounding it into a powder. Molasses is stirred in, along with
cinnamon, cloves, and ginger, and the mixture is sealed in an
earthenware crock and left to steam slowly in the oven for two days
and two nights. Syrnikov's insistence on the deliciousness of the
most basic preparations—which often call for less than a handful of
ingredients—offers a corrective to the belief that the Russian peasant diet was completely dull. It was admittedly monotonous, but it
had distinct pleasures. Syrnikov's books offer an unabashed celebration of Russian folk life and aim to rekindle pride in the country's culinary culture.

In 2014 an activist youth group called "Eat Russian" began
staging publicity stunts in which they raided grocery stores where
they "discovered" foreign products that were imported in apparent
violation of the counter-sanctions Russia had imposed against
Western foodstuffs. Denouncing imported food as dangerous, the
group insists that "Russian means real." Culinary nationalism also
underlies the new chain of food shops cum cafés called Let's Eat
Like at Home (*Edim kak doma*) conceived by the renowned film-
maker brothers Andrei Konchalovsky and Nikita Mikhalkov. The
project is a spin-off from the hugely popular cooking show *Let's Eat
at Home!* (*Edim doma!*) hosted by Konchalovsky's wife, Julia
Vysotskaya. In 2015 the Kremlin-friendly brothers asked the government for nearly one billion rubles up front to support their venture, positioning it as a much-needed alternative to McDonald's,
which they painted as "hostile to the Russian spirit." The announce-
ment of their project set off a firestorm of mockery on social media,

FIGURE 16. Alexander Miridonov, Raid organized in a Moscow supermarket by activists from the "Eat Russian" movement, 2015. The group invited journalists to witness the raid, in which they denounced foreign foods and placed stickers depicting a Russian bear roaring at the American flag on foods allegedly imported in violation of the counter-sanctions Russia imposed following the annexation of Crimea. Kommersant Photo.

with one Twitter user posting a parody of the new burger's components that showed the highest percentage of ingredients to be 46 percent "spirituality." Although Putin was said to have liked the project, he stopped short of government investment, promising instead strong bureaucratic support. Even without Kremlin funds the project eventually came to fruition, with franchises launching in 2019. Customers choose from a small menu that, save for two types of pasta, is composed entirely of Russian comfort foods. Each order is cooked quickly sous vide for consumption on site, or it can be packed for takeout. The ingredients are billed as "natural" and *otechestvennye,* a loaded word that refers to domestic production but that carries connotations of jingoistic patriotism, like the Great Patriotic War, which is Russia's name for World War II.

What Is to Come

In 1990 the Soviet Union's first independent television station aired a new comedy show called *Oba-na!* (Here We Go!), shortly before McDonald's opened in Moscow. The pilot episode, "The Funeral of Food," featured a mock procession that parodied the somber funerals of Soviet leaders, except that the deceased was the food that had disappeared from the city's shelves. The campy delivery did not veil the episode's pointed message. Twenty-five years later, when shops were once again empty of food following the bans against imported products, the episode was revived on social media. Although the comic performance still resonated, much had changed in the intervening years. The 1990s brought a surge of foreign imports and the opening of hundreds of restaurants in which the brusque service of Soviet times gave way to a customer-oriented approach. The once-bare shelves of squalid state stores were replaced by upscale groceries carrying ingredients rarefied enough to please oligarchs' palates, even if many of these shelves were again temporarily bare. The grand Eliseev grocery managed to survive revolution, war, shortages, and, most recently, the pandemic. When the store's closing was announced in March 2021, the uproar was so great that the Moscow city government moved to take over the property and vowed to protect the store as a cultural monument.

In the twenty-first century Russia has moved from being an importer of wheat to the world's largest wheat exporter, sending nearly 34.5 million tons onto the world market in 2019–2020. The wheat grown for export is not the product of small farms, however. Just ten companies account for over 50 percent of these exports, and the power and reach of corporate agriculture will only increase if improvements to Russia's weak infrastructure are carried out as planned. Climate change will likely open up farmland for growing wheat in more northerly regions, and shipping patterns are poised to change, too. One ambitious plan involves the recent completion of a new grain terminal at the small port of Zarubino on the Sea of Japan, only eleven miles from the Chinese border. The ice-free harbor is connected with multiple rail lines that can facilitate the transport of grain to China, Korea, and Japan.

Such abundant wheat production means no shortage of cattle feed and plenty of grain for human consumption; the exports bring in much-needed foreign currency besides. But there is a downside to the drive to boost the wheat harvest: the loss of rye. Beginning with the push for mechanization in the late 1920s, collective farm workers found that combines had trouble harvesting rye, which grows considerably taller than wheat. So when possible, they cultivated wheat instead. Already in Soviet times some commentators were ruing the disappearance of rye as Russia's predominant grain, believing that it eroded Russian national identity in a country that for centuries had defined itself as "the kingdom of rye." For many, the post-Soviet desire for white breads like baguettes and airy buns only deepened the cultural loss.

Russia's evolving "food revolution" is shaped not only by consumer demand but also by politics beyond the consumer's control. In a new twist on the old Slavophile versus Westernizer debate, the political pundit Nikolai Troitsky has suggested that the main reason for Russia's counter-sanctions against foreign food was Putin's desire to paint the country's liberals as retrogrades dependent on oysters and prosciutto. These sanctions, however, were distasteful not only to the country's elite but also to Russia's new middle class, who now had the means to eat out and indulge their personal tastes by experimenting with unfamiliar cuisines or choosing healthier foods.

Restaurant culture continues to change. Where theme restaurants like Turandot that opened early in the millennium focused primarily on ambience, more recent culinary ventures concentrate on the quality of their food. Russia now has its share of celebrity chefs, mainly in Moscow, where two restaurants, White Rabbit and Twins Garden, made the list of the World's 50 Best Restaurants in 2019, both placing in the top twenty. The mission of White Rabbit's chef, Vladimir Mukhin, is to bring Russian cuisine to the larger world. In striving to identify the quintessential flavors and techniques of the Russian kitchen and present them in contemporary form, he hopes to emulate the global impact of New Nordic food. In 2016 Mukhin opened the White Rabbit Lab, modeled on the experimental laboratory of taste pioneered by the famous Copenhagen restaurant Noma. There he worked up a tasting menu called "Forward into the Past," based on ingredients mentioned in the sixteenth-century *Domostroi* but executed in his own style, in recipes he devised himself. Swan's liver and elk's lips seem designed more for their shock value than for any sustained resurrection of old Russian foodways, but the menu overall featured the bold, distinctive flavors that Russians love. At Twins Garden, the twin Berezutskiy brothers similarly aim to astonish the palate—not surprisingly, given that Ivan Berezutskiy interned under the boundary-pushing Spanish chef Ferran Adrià, while Sergei staged at Grant Achatz's inventive Chicago restaurant Alinea. Like White

Rabbit, Twins Garden focuses on Russian practice, though it is more overtly concerned with the local and seasonal: around 70 percent of the menu features produce from the restaurant's own farm. One of its tasting menus, called simply "Vegetables," carries the idea of a plant-based meal to the extreme, making use of vegetables at all stages of their life cycle, from seeds to peelings. Even the accompanying house wines have been produced from vegetables, mushrooms, and herbs. Another tasting menu, titled "Rediscover Russia," offers an education in regional foods as it carries diners across Russia's vast expanse, from the far north to the far east and into the warmer climes of the south. Although ordinary Russians rarely frequent these cutting-edge restaurants, their focus on Russian cuisine has influenced a range of less exclusive venues, as ever more places open with the promise of "real" Russian food. Moscow's Uhvat is a good example. Its name refers to the large tongs that are used to insert and retrieve pots from the masonry stove. All of the dishes on the menu are prepared in one of its three traditional stoves; even butter is melted in them.

Throughout Russia's history, its cuisine has been enriched by any number of adoptions and adaptations of ingredients and dishes from both East and West. Tea and dumplings arrived early from China. Imperial Russia witnessed the ascendancy of French cooking techniques that introduced small cuts of meat, heavy cream sauces, and elaborate, butter-rich pastries. The Soviet Union welcomed dishes from culinary cultures stretching from Central Asia to the Baltic Sea. Post-Soviet Russia embraced American fast food along with novel foods from across the globe, and then sent its Russian burgers back to Los Angeles and Brighton Beach. So what might be in store in the coming decades? As Vladimir Mukhin declared in 2016 at the Chefs Revolution, a Dutch avant-garde festival of cuisine, "National culture is the future of gastronomy." Chefs may resurrect old recipes and tweak them into new forms, as Mukhin does in his restaurants, but even in the most forward-looking dishes, certain elemental Russian tastes remain constant: the sour note of fermented foods, found in lacto-fermented pickles, brined fruits, traditional rye bread, and kvass; the earthy flavors of wild mushrooms and buckwheat groats; the zesty bite of horseradish and mustard; soups enlivened with souring agents like kvass and pickle brine; the tart tang of Antonov apples and sea buckthorn; the sweet allure of honey and of milk baked to caramelized silkiness. Russia's ancient foodways were created from practices born of hardship and hunger. Today they are being renewed with imagination and vigor, opening not a window on the West but a new window onto a culinary and cultural past that connects meaningfully with the future.

Acknowledgments

This book has emerged from fifty-odd years of thinking about Russia and food. I have learned so much from so many people who shared their expertise with me, and often their recipes. First among them is my dear friend Nadezhda Shokhen, who continues to enlighten me to this day. I am also indebted to Kate Marshall, my editor at the University of California Press, for her enthusiasm and steadfast support. Thanks, too, to the director of the Press, Tim Sullivan, whose encouragement jumpstarted this book; to Enrique Ochoa-Kaup for expertly shepherding the manuscript through production; and to Erika Bűky for her sensitive copyediting.

I couldn't have completed my research during the pandemic without the invaluable help of Alison O'Grady at Williams College's Interlibrary Loan service and of Jan Adamczyk at University of Illinois's Slavic Reference Service. The photographs that enrich this book could only have been arranged with the assistance of Sonya and Anatol Bekkerman and Tatiana Sosnora, as well as the prodigious efforts of Olga Sviblova and Mikhail Krasnov at the Multimedia Art Museum in Moscow, Natalia Kopaneva at Saint Petersburg's Kunstkamera, and Natalia Zhukova at Moscow's State Historical Museum. Thanks also to Polina Nazarenko of Rossiya

Segodnya/Sputnik. My Williams colleague Olga Shevchenko was truly heroic in her months-long efforts to help me secure the cover image for the book.

I am grateful to have enormously gifted friends and colleagues who read my manuscript and offered astute and generous comments. Thanks go to Angela Brintlinger, Helena Goscilo, Olga Shevchenko, Amy Trubek, and Jenny Wapner. For all of the books I've written, I've been blessed with the very best editor possible, my husband, Dean Crawford, who reads every word I write, works magic on twisted phrases, and most important of all, has accompanied me on my wild Russian journey for over forty years now. My gratitude and love, always.

Suggestions for Further Reading

Baron, Samuel H., ed. *The Travels of Olearius in Seventeenth-Century Russia.* Stanford, CA: Stanford University Press, 1967.

Boym, Constantin. "My McDonald's." *Gastronomica: The Journal of Food and Culture,* February 2001.

Caldwell, Melissa L. *Dacha Idylls: Living Organically in Russia's Countryside.* Berkeley: University of California Press, 2010.

Chekhov, Anton. "Oysters." In *Chekhov: The Early Stories, 1883–1888,* translated by Patrick Miles and Harvey Pitcher. New York: Macmillan, 1982.

Chekhov, Anton. "The Siren." In *Chekhov: The Comic Stories,* translated by Harvey Pitcher. Chicago: Ivan R. Dee, 1999.

Dinner Is Served: The Russian Museum Culinary Companion. Saint Petersburg: The Russian Museum/Palace Editions, 2013.

Engelgardt, Aleksandr Nikolaevich. *Letters from the Country, 1872–1887.* Translated by Cathy A. Frierson. Oxford: Oxford University Press, 1993.

Ginzburg, Lidiya. *Blockade Diary.* Translated by Alan Myers. London: The Harvill Press, 1995.

Glants, Musya, and Joyce Toomre, eds. *Food in Russian History and Culture.* Bloomington: Indiana University Press, 1997.

Gogol, Nikolai. "Old-World Landowners." In *The Collected Tales of Nikolai Gogol,* edited by Leonard J. Kent. New York: Pantheon Books, 1964.

Goldstein, Darra. "Hot Prospekts: Dining in the New Russia." In *Celebrity and Glamour in Contemporary Russia: Shocking Chic,* edited by Helena Goscilo and Vlad Strukov. Abingdon, UK: Routledge, 2010.

Goldstein, Darra. *Beyond the North Wind: Russia in Recipes and Lore.* California/New York: Ten Speed Press, 2020.

Goldstein, Darra. *A Taste of Russia.* 3rd ed. Montpelier, VT: RIS Publications, 2012.

Goldstein, Darra. "Theatre of the Gastronomic Absurd." *Performance Research* 4, no. 1 (1999).

Goldstein, Darra. "Women under Siege: Leningrad 1941–1942." In *From Betty Crocker to Feminist Food Studies: Critical Perspectives on Women and Food,* edited by Arlene Voski Avakian and Barbara Haber. Amherst: University of Massachusetts Press, 2005.

Gronow, Jukka. *Caviar with Champagne: Common Luxury and the Ideals of the Good Life in Stalin's Russia.* Oxford: Berg, 2003.

Lakhtikova, Anastasia, Angela Brintlinger, and Irina Glushchenko, eds. *Seasoned Socialism: Gender and Food in Late Soviet Everyday Life.* Bloomington: Indiana University Press, 2019.

LeBlanc, Ronald D. *Slavic Sins of the Flesh: Food, Sex, and Carnal Appetite in Nineteenth-Century Russian Fiction.* Durham: University of New Hampshire Press, 2009.

Molokhovets, Elena. *Classic Russian Cooking.* Translated by Joyce Toomre. Bloomington: Indiana University Press, 1998.

Pouncy, Carolyn Johnson, ed. *The Domostroi: Rules for Russian Households in the Time of Ivan the Terrible.* Ithaca: Cornell University Press, 1994.

Ries, Nancy. "Potato Ontology: Surviving Postsocialism in Russia." *Cultural Anthropology* 24, no. 2 (2009).

Roosevelt, Priscilla. *Life on the Russian Country Estate: A Social and Cultural History.* New Haven, CT: Yale University Press, 1995.

Russian Fairy Tales. Collected by Aleksandr Afanas'ev. Translated by Norbert Guterman. New York: Pantheon Books, 1945.

Schrad, Mark Lawrence. *Vodka Politics: Alcohol, Autocracy, and the Secret History of the Russian State.* New York: Oxford University Press, 2016.

Smith, R. E. F., and David Christian. *Bread and Salt: A Social and Economic History of Food and Drink in Russia.* Cambridge: Cambridge University Press, 1984.

Sorokin, Vladimir. "Farewell to the Queue," Words without Borders, September 2008, http://wordswithoutborders.org/article/farewell-to-the-queue.

Trutter, Marion, ed. *Culinaria Russia: A Celebration of Food and Tradition.* Potsdam: H. F. Ullmann publishing, 2013.

Vapnyar, Lara. *Broccoli and Other Tales of Food and Love.* New York: Pantheon Books, 2008.

Wasson, Valentina Pavlovna, and R. Gordon. *Mushrooms, Russia and History.* New York: Pantheon Books, 1957.

Index

fireweed tea, 39

fish and fish dishes, 16, 37, 48–49, 53, 80, 98; dried and salted fish, 42, 48; *kulebiaka,* 7, 15, 95, 112, 114; *stroganina,* 47; *ukha,* 14. *See also* caviar; sturgeon

fishing industry and trade, 28, 80

flours: birch bark, 65; oat *(tolokno),* 5, 12, 142; pea flour, 69. *See also* bread; grains; *specific grains*

folk beliefs and traditions, 10, 19–20, 33, 67–68; bread and salt presentation, 95–96, 115

folktales, 6, 42–43

food acquisition: bartering, 50, 82, 86, 134; grocery stores and shopping, 82–88, 124, 137–38, 142, 144–45, 146; healthfulness/quality and, 136–37; hunting and fishing, 16. *See also* foraging; gardens

food and drink introductions, 12–13, 16, 26–31, 49–50, 51. *See also* foreign foods and beverages

food distribution: and food insecurity, in Soviet Russia, 2, 4, 50–51, 73, 78, 83; and the Volga famine of 1891, 65. *See also* food acquisition

food insecurity and famines, 2, 4, 63–94; causative factors, 2, 4, 64, 65, 70, 78–79; church dietary dictates and fast-day foods, 5–6, 48–49, 68–69; famine foods, 65–66, 75–76, 76*fig.,* 77; the famine of 1921–1922, 69–71; fatalism about, 5, 67–68; food insecurity and social status, 77–78; hospitality and, 122–23; in

post-Soviet Russia, 92, 134–35; the practice of begging for crusts, 66–67; private gardens and, 73–74, 89–92, 134–35; response to destruction of EU food imports (2015), 63–64; ubiquity in Russian history, 64–65; vegetarianism proposed as solution for, 51–52; the Volga famine of 1891, 65, 67. *See also* scarcity/abundance; Soviet-era food shortages

food preparation. *See* cooking and preserving methods; cooking and serving equipment; home cooking

food preservation, xvii–xviii, 12, 27; curing and salting, 41–46; drying, 33, 48; fermentation and culturing, 33, 38–41; freezing, 46–47

food rationing, 75, 76*fig.,* 88–89; *payok* (special rations), 60, 86

foraging and foraged foods, 10, 12, 89, 136, 142; in times of food insecurity, 51–52, 65, 77. *See also specific foods*

foreign foods and beverages: adoption and influence of, 5, 13, 16, 54, 149–50; current attitudes about, 140–46, 147–48; imports and foreign foods in Soviet Russia, 79, 85, 86, 87–88; post-Soviet bans on foreign imports, 63–64, 146, 147–48; renewed focus on domestically-produced foods, 141–46. *See also* food and drink introductions; luxury foods and beverages; trade and trade routes; *specific foods*

hospitality, 95–123; bread and salt as symbol of, 95–96, 115; cultural importance of, 94, 96, 122–23, 139; food insecurity and, 122–23; foreigners' views of Russian hospitality, 97–99, 106–7, 108–9, 111; the kissing ritual, 106–7; moral/religious ideas about, 101–2, 103*fig.*, 104–5; open tables, 102, 104; in peasant homes, 96; *podacha*s in medieval Russia, 97; the primacy of traditional foods and flavors, 114; published advice about, 25–26, 105, 107; Russian-style table service, 98, 99, 110–14; Russian words for, 95, 96; in Soviet Russia, xvii, 94, 107, 121–23; teatime rituals, 115–21; toward strangers, 96, 102, 104; wealthy/aristocratic, lavishness of, 16, 96, 97–104, 113–14; wealthy/aristocratic dining aesthetics, 108–10, 111, 112, 113

Hotel du Nord (Saint Petersburg), 58

hunger. *See* food insecurity; scarcity/abundance; Soviet-era food shortages

"Hunger" (Khlebnikov), 70–71

hunting and fishing, 16; fishing industry and trade, 28, 80

ice cream, 85

icehouses, 47

illusion and trompe l'oeil, 6, 81, 82, 99, 109–10, 113–14, 130–31

Imperial Porcelain Factory, 109

imported foods and beverages. *See* food and drink introductions; foreign foods and beverages; trade and trade routes

Ivan IV (the Terrible), 24, 27, 43

Ivan tea, 39

jam, 36, 90*fig.*

John Chrysostom, Saint, 102

Journey to Arzrum (Pushkin), 18

kabaki, 57

Kadyrov, Ramzan, 133

kalach, 56, 62

Kaluga dough, 4–5, 23*fig.*

kasha, 13, 51, 67, 114

kefir, 41

KFC, 130

kharchevni, 57

khleb da sol', 95–96

Khlebnikov, Velimir, 70–71

Khrushchev, Nikita, 79–80

kisel', 11–12, 56, 69

kislye shchi, 22, 114

kitchens: factory kitchens, 58–60, 59*fig.*; home and communal kitchens, 92–94, 93*fig.*, 121–22

kombucha, 39–40

Konchalovsky, Andrei, 144–45

korchmy, 56–57

Kostrovitskaia, Vera, 122

koumiss, 27

kroshevo, 143–44

kukhmisterskie, 57, 58

kulaga, 69

kulaks, 71–72

kulebiaka, 7, 15, 95, 112, 114

kulich, 116*fig.*

kulinariia, 84

kundiumy, 35

Moscow: early restaurants in, 58; McDonald's opening in, 61, 124–26, 125*fig.*; the Narkomfin House, 122; post-Soviet, restaurants in, 126–33, 148–49; private garden plots in, 134; Soviet-era food shopping in, 83–88, 124

Mukhin, Vladimir, 148, 149–50

Muscovy Company, 28

mushrooms, 11, 12, 38, 48, 89, 114

mustard, 5, 17, 38, 139

Nabokov, Vladimir, 10

Napoleon, 22, 23*fig.*

Narkomfin House (Moscow), 122

Narpit, 50

National Cuisines of Our Peoples, The (Pokhlyobkin), 31

nationalism, culinary, 23*fig.*, 30–31, 104, 126–27, 130, 143–46, 147

nature, Russians' connections to, 10, 16, 135. *See also* foraging; gardens

necrophagy, 70

New Economic Policy (NEP), 71

Nicholas I, 25

Noma, 148

Nordman-Severova, Natalia, 51–52

Norenskaya Poetic Potato festival, 136

Norwegian trade, 29

Notes of a Provincial Wildfowler (Aksakov), 16

Notes on Fishing (Aksakov), 16

Novikov, Arkady, 132

nutrition. *See* health and nutrition

oats and oatmeal, 4–5, 11–12, 51; *kisel'*, 11–12, 56

obzhornye riady, 57

oils and fats, 12, 13, 16, 38, 47, 52–53, 68, 69

Old Way of Life, The (Pyliaev), 99, 100, 101

"Old-World Landowners" (Gogol), 25

Olearius, Adam, 45, 106–7

onions, 13, 89

Onishchenko, Gennady, 126–27

On the Corruption of Morals in Russia (Shcherbatov), 104

open tables, 102, 104

organic foods and farming, 137–38

ovens, 33; traditional masonry stoves, 31–34, 32*fig.*, 35

ovinnik, 67

"Oysters" (Chekhov), 66–67

pan-frying, 37–38

pastila, 12

pastries. *See* pies; sweets and pastries

payok (special food rations), 60, 86

peas, dried, 69

peasant diet and foodways, 17, 19, 52–53; church dietary dictates and fast-day foods, 48, 68–69; food access inequities, 2, 16, 86; hospitality, 96; the impacts of collectivization, 72, 73–74; introduced foods and, 49–50, 51; private gardens, 73–74, 89–92; renewed appreciation of, 143–44; in times of famine, 65–67; use of the samovar, 37*fig.*, 119–20. *See also* social status; traditional foods and foodways

pel'meni, 27–28, 47, 61

Pepsi and PepsiCo, 22, 24

perestroika, 88–89, 107, 127–28

Peter the Great, 29–30, 57, 89–90, 99; impacts on Russian culinary culture, 16, 21, 30, 49, 107, 108, 111

Petrograd, 121. *See also* Saint Petersburg

Pevzner, Manuil, 50

Piancone, Louis, Sr., 127–28, 128*fig.*

pickle brine, 14, 38

pickles, 38, 51, 85–86, 112. *See also* fermented foods

pies, 15–16, 15*fig.*, 37, 56, 112, 121; *kulebiaka,* 7, 15, 95, 112, 114

pineapple, 110

Pineapples in Champagne (Severianin), 110

pirozhki, 56

pishcha/eda distinction, 51, 127

pizza, 127–29, 128*fig.*, 141

Pizza Hut, 128–29

poaching, 37

*podacha*s, 97

Pokhlyobkin, Vil'yam, 31

polevik, 67

Pomors, 29

Popov porcelain factory, 109

porcelain tableware, 109

porridges and gruels, 11, 12, 13, 33, 51, 69; *kisel',* 11–12, 56, 69

post-Soviet Russia, 124–50; agriculture in, 137, 141–42, 146–47; chain restaurants in, 56, 61, 124–30, 132–33, 144–45, 149; economic change and uncertainty in, 126, 133–34, 137–38; economic sanctions and foreign import bans, 63–64, 142, 145*fig.*, 146,

147–48; food insecurity in, 92, 134–35; higher-end restaurants and recent restaurant trends, 61–62, 130–31, 142–43, 146, 148–49; the loss of the queue, 124; nostalgia for Soviet-era foods and service, 60, 131–32; renewed focus on traditional and domestically-produced foods, 140–46, 148–50

potatoes, 13, 56, 75, 78; cultural importance of, 89, 134, 135–36; introduction and adoption of, 49–50, 89

pots and pans, 34

prianiki (gingerbread), 1–2, 3*fig.*, 11, 23*fig.*

probiotics, 41. *See also* cultured foods and beverages; fermented foods and beverages

produce, 12–13; at farmer's markets, 85; garden-grown, 73–74, 82, 89–92, 134–36. *See also* agriculture; *specific types*

"Puffed Rice and Meatballs" (Vapnyar), 87–88

Pushkin, Alexander, 18, 22, 39

Putin, Vladimir, 63, 133, 145, 147–48

Pyliaev, Mikhail, 99, 100, 101

rationing of food, 75, 76*fig.*, 88–89; special rations *(payok),* 60, 86

Real Russian Food (Syrnikov), 143, 144

recipes. *See* cookbooks and recipes

Repin, Ilya, 52

restaurants and taverns, 16, 56–62, 124–33, 148–50; cafeterias and canteens in Soviet Russia, 58–60,

California Studies in Food and Culture

DARRA GOLDSTEIN, EDITOR

Founded in 1893,
UNIVERSITY OF CALIFORNIA PRESS
publishes bold, progressive books and journals
on topics in the arts, humanities, social sciences,
and natural sciences—with a focus on social
justice issues—that inspire thought and action
among readers worldwide.

The UC PRESS FOUNDATION
raises funds to uphold the press's vital role
as an independent, nonprofit publisher, and
receives philanthropic support from a wide
range of individuals and institutions—and from
committed readers like you. To learn more, visit
ucpress.edu/supportus.